THE HQ TRAINING MANUAL

THE (UNOFFICIAL) GUIDE

TO WINNING

AMERICA'S HOTTEST TRIVIA GAME

JOHN B. CLARK

PERMUTED PRESS

A PERMUTED PRESS BOOK

ISBN: 978-1-68261-837-0
ISBN (eBook): 978-1-68261-838-7

The HQ Training Manual:
The (Unofficial) Guide to Winning America's Hottest
Trivia Game
© 2018 by Permuted Press
All Rights Reserved

Cover art by Cody Corcoran

PERMUTED
PRESS

Permuted Press, LLC
New York • Nashville
permutedpress.com

Published in the United States of America

There's nothing quite like settling around the phone at 3:00 or 9:00 p.m. to compete against a million or so fellow HQuties. The prize money is great, but more often than not, the bragging rights are what one is after, emerging victorious along with a handful of others.

The game is difficult—there are 12 questions to answer and only 10 seconds to answer each. After the first two no-brainers, things ramp up pretty quickly. Some quizzes are exceptionally challenging while some contain merely a couple of truly difficult questions. Nevertheless, getting all 12 questions correct without the benefit of an extra life is hard and often requires some luck, as every quiz requires a certain amount of guessing.

I've created this training manual to help you prepare your brain for the daily grind of competition and to give you a leg up going forward. I've subtracted the 2 questions at the top to give you 72 ten-question quizzes that approximate the experience of the *HQ* quiz. The questions range from easy to hard to very difficult, though each quiz is unique. I cover a broad range of categories, from pop culture to politics, science to sports, and many things in between.

Grab your pencil and start quizzing. In this book, there's no clock. Keep count of your correct answers and assess your average of correct responses—5 to 6 correct answers is the average. At that level, you're a good competitor consistently finishing shy of the prize. Maintain an average of 7 to 8 correct answers and you're operating at a high level. Anything above that is elite and suggests you're on the verge of taking home some of that purse.

Most of all, have fun and remember that any incorrect answer here only results in your learning something new. Every question in this book is a little bit of knowledge for you to tuck in your brain to unpack sometime in the future!

Quiz answers begin on page 167. I recommend doing two quizzes at a time as the answers appear on facing pages. This will reduce the risk of accidentally "cheating" by seeing the answers to a quiz you've not yet taken.

Enjoy!

—*John B. Clark*

QUIZ 1

1. **For what was Daryl Hannah arrested in August 2011 in Washington, D.C.?**
   ① Jaywalking
   ② Unpaid parking tickets
   ③ Protesting on the White House property

2. **Which of the 4 competitive racing strokes is characterized by swimming on one's back?**
   ① Breaststroke
   ② Backstroke
   ③ Freestyle

3. **Who wrote the 1979 book *The Hitchhiker's Guide to the Galaxy*?**
   ① Douglas Adams
   ② Jack London
   ③ Ayn Rand

4. **Who gave Spain claim to Florida by exploring St. Augustine?**
   ① John Smith
   ② Juan Ponce de León
   ③ Jacques Cartier

5. **Art Deco was a movement focusing on what element of art?**
   ① Decorative
   ② Size
   ③ Motion

6. **Who began hosting MSNBC's political forum *Hardball* in 1999?**

   ① Wolf Blitzer
   ② Larry King
   ③ Chris Matthews

7. **What was the first single from Alicia Keys' album *Diary of Alicia Keys*?**

   ① "You Don't Know My Name"
   ② "A Woman's Worth"
   ③ "Fallin'"

8. **In *The Lord of the Rings*, what is the name of Bilbo's blade that he passed on to Frodo?**

   ① Arure
   ② Sting
   ③ Glint

9. **Which 14-time PGA Tour winner was the 2011 Champions Tour Rookie of the Year?**

   ① Chip Beck
   ② Mark Calcavecchia
   ③ Kenny Perry

10. **Which president of the Soviet Union died in 1953, at the age of 73?**

    ① Stalin
    ② Brezhnev
    ③ Khrushchev

HQUIZZING TIP

A great way to play and carve a path to victory is to assemble a team of friends and family. The more people available to contribute, the better your chances of getting the answer correct. Share the glory!

QUIZ 2

1. **Which famous quote is not attributed to baseball great Yogi Berra?**

   ① "The future ain't what it used to be."
   ② "You can observe a lot by watching."
   ③ "I'm smarter than the average bear."

2. **What process changes a rock's chemical composition to break it down?**

   ① Chemical weathering
   ② Icicle weathering
   ③ Physical weathering

3. **Which woman started The Fresh Air Fund?**

   ① Celine Dion
   ② Mariah Carey
   ③ Shania Twain

4. **In the movie *Star Wars*, to whom does Darth Vader say, "I find your lack of faith disturbing"?**

   ① Captain Needa
   ② Grand Moff Tarkin
   ③ Admiral Motti

5. **Avril Lavigne was born and raised in what country?**

   ① United States
   ② Canada
   ③ France

6. **The most striking element of Paul Cézanne's eye-catching paintings was his use of what?**

   ① Black
   ② Color
   ③ Graphite

7. **Anheuser-Busch survived prohibition by selling commercial yeast and what?**

   ① Root beer
   ② Soda pop
   ③ Sarsaparilla

8. **In which country would the word "strand" mean an actual beach?**

   ① Cuba
   ② Germany
   ③ Italy

9. **The term "googly" is used in which sport?**

   ① Cricket
   ② Rugby
   ③ Polo

10. **Cephalgia is a medical term for what malady?**

    ① Dizziness
    ② Earache
    ③ Headache

QUIZ 3

1. **Which 1980s cartoon series was made into a feature film in 2011?**
   - ① *The Snorks*
   - ② *The Smurfs*
   - ③ *Voltron*

2. **What is the name of Sherlock Holmes' brother?**
   - ① Mycroft
   - ② Marcel
   - ③ Evelyn

3. **How wide is the average person's field of vision?**
   - ① 90 degrees
   - ② 8 miles
   - ③ 180 degrees

4. **Who wrote the book *True Speed: My Racing Life*?**
   - ① Dale Earnhardt Jr.
   - ② Tony Stewart
   - ③ Jeff Gordon

5. **In which country was Dolly, the first sheep cloned from adult sheep cells, born?**
   - ① Ireland
   - ② Scotland
   - ③ Austria

6. **Iconic *Vogue* editor Anna Wintour was satirized in which hit movie?**
   ① *The Devil Wears Prada*
   ② *Zoolander*
   ③ *Mean Girls*

7. **In which country would one find the largest concentration of impact craters due to meteoroids?**
   ① Siberia
   ② Russia
   ③ Canada

8. **Japanese archery is called what?**
   ① Kyūdō
   ② Kobudō
   ③ Nage-waza

9. **What is the title of Johnny Cash's 1986 novel?**
   ① *I Walk the Line*
   ② *Man in White*
   ③ *Ring of Fire*

10. **The poem that opens *Twilight: Breaking Dawn Part 1* is by which poet?**
    ① Edgar Allen Poe
    ② Robert Frost
    ③ Edna St. Vincent Millay

QUIZ 4

1. **Annabella Lwin was the singer for which 1980s musical group?**
   - ① Bananarama
   - ② Blondie
   - ③ Bow Wow Wow

2. ***Rocky* won an Academy Award for best film in which year?**
   - ① 1956
   - ② 1976
   - ③ 1979

3. **Which Italian artist was the first to abandon the Byzantine style and paint more lifelike characters?**
   - ① Giotto
   - ② Gauguin
   - ③ Cézanne

4. **What makes a martini "dirty"?**
   - ① Diluted with ice
   - ② Olive brine
   - ③ Vodka

5. **Which Greek goddess was depicted in a 30-foot statue near the Acropolis?**
   - ① Athena
   - ② Aphrodite
   - ③ Hera

6. **How long did Dickens take to write *A Christmas Carol*?**
    ① 2 months
    ② 2 weeks
    ③ 2 years

7. **What light-sensitive cells in the eye detect colors?**
    ① Pupils
    ② Cones
    ③ Irises

8. **When did the San Francisco Giants play their last game at Candlestick Park?**
    ① 2000
    ② 2001
    ③ 1999

9. **As it relates to Wall Street, what is the opposite of a "liquid market"?**
    ① Firm market
    ② Thin market
    ③ Solid market

10. **On *The Simpsons*, what is Sideshow Bob's middle name?**
    ① Terwilliger
    ② Palmerston
    ③ Underdunk

QUIZ 5

1. **Which blood type is the universal donor?**
   ① A
   ② B
   ③ O

2. **In baseball, what's meant by the term "can of corn"?**
   ① Sacrifice bunt
   ② High pop fly
   ③ A play off the outfield wall

3. ***Dancing with the Stars* judge Carrie Ann Inaba was a dancer on what popular 1990s television show?**
   ① *Rap City*
   ② *In Living Color*
   ③ *The Arsenio Hall Show*

4. ***The Birdcage* starring Robin Williams is a remake of which film?**
   ① *La Cage aux Folles*
   ② *Teacher's Pet*
   ③ *Breathless*

5. **Who was The Beatles' "girl with kaleidoscope eyes"?**
   ① "Lovely Rita"
   ② "Polythene Pam"
   ③ "Lucy in the Sky with Diamonds"

6. **What did the first vending machine dispense?**
   ① Holy water
   ② Stamps
   ③ Chewing gum

7. **Which vegetable has the highest sugar content?**
   ① Potato
   ② Onion
   ③ Tomato

8. **What was a leather-covered golf ball stuffed with feathers called?**
   ① The Featherie
   ② The Gutta-Percha
   ③ The Bramble

9. **Demi Lovato began her acting career appearing on what children's television show at age 6?**
   ① *The Wiggles*
   ② *Teletubbies*
   ③ *Barney & Friends*

10. **Which pair of characters is from the 2005 film *Hostage*?**
    ① Reed Richards and Johnny Storm
    ② Will Stronghold and The Commander
    ③ Jeff Talley and Walter Smith

QUIZ 6 (SPORTS)

1. **How many KOs did Muhammad Ali have in his career?**
   ① 29
   ② 37
   ③ 41

2. **In 2012 what NFL team called LP Field stadium their home?**
   ① Pittsburgh Steelers
   ② Buffalo Bills
   ③ Tennessee Titans

3. **In roller derby, what refers to the mass of blockers from both teams within 10 feet of one other?**
   ① Flock
   ② Pack
   ③ Mob

4. **In 2014, which golfer won 3 times in 8 starts, after previously going 187 events without a victory?**
   ① Jimmy Walker
   ② Rickie Fowler
   ③ Chris Kirk

5. **Who won the Conn Smythe Trophy as the 2011–12 NHL Playoff MVP?**
   ① Anze Kopitar
   ② Jonathon Quick
   ③ Matt Greene

6. **Jarkko Nieminen's wife, Anu Weckstrom, is the #1 Finnish player in which sport?**
   ① Badminton
   ② Squash
   ③ Tennis

7. **Which women's Olympic basketball team won bronze in Atlanta and silver in Sydney?**
   ① Germany
   ② Canada
   ③ Australia

8. **Dikembe Mutombo missed 2 weeks in the 2000 season for which ailment?**
   ① Poison ivy
   ② Malaria
   ③ Pink eye

9. **On May 22, 2007, which city was named host to the 2011 Super Bowl?**
   ① Arlington
   ② Chicago
   ③ Detroit

10. **In what year were two-litre rules introduced in Formula 3 racing?**
    ① 1979
    ② 1967
    ③ 1974

QUIZ 7

1. **Kate Hudson is the daughter of which famous actress?**
   ① Sissy Spacek
   ② Goldie Hawn
   ③ Kathleen Turner

2. **On which album cover appears a picture of a New York apartment building?**
   ① *Houses of the Holy*
   ② *Led Zeppelin III*
   ③ *Physical Graffiti*

3. **Which flag can be seen prominently in the Delacroix painting *Liberty Leading the People*?**
   ① The Fleur de Lis flag of France
   ② The Union Jack
   ③ The French Tricolour

4. **Cabernet Sauvignon is known as the king of red grapes; which varietal is known as the queen?**
   ① Pinot Noir
   ② Zinfandel
   ③ Barbera

5. **What is the northernmost capital city in the world?**
   ① Reykjavik, Iceland
   ② Ottawa, Canada
   ③ Moscow, Russia

6. **Who is the first Minnesota Twins pitcher to have won 2 Cy Young Awards?**
   ① Bert Blyleven
   ② Johan Santana
   ③ Jim Kaat

7. **In which city did Jennifer Hudson audition for *American Idol*?**
   ① Atlanta
   ② Houston
   ③ New York

8. **The show *It's Always Sunny in Philadelphia* features which 2 characters?**
   ① Jim Tisnewski and Colonel McNulty
   ② Nathan Templeton and Jim Gardner
   ③ Charlie and Dennis

9. **Which artist was the son of a racehorse trainer?**
   ① Francis Bacon
   ② Jackson Pollock
   ③ Edgar Degas

10. **Which publication uses the slogan "The Daily Diary of the American Dream"?**
    ① *The New York Times*
    ② *Bloomberg Businessweek*
    ③ *The Wall Street Journal*

H-QUIZZING TIP

There are times when the question is so difficult or obscure, you won't have any idea what the answer is. Instead of choosing the "likeliest" answer in your mind, go for the unlikeliest and hope for the best. Oftentimes, the counterintuitive route is the winning route.

QUIZ 8

1. **Which events combine with swimming to form a triathlon?**

    ① Long jump and pole vault
    ② Running and cycling
    ③ Fencing and equestrian

2. **Which of these famous sidekicks was *not* on *The Howard Stern Show*?**

    ① Hank the Angry Dwarf
    ② Silent Bob
    ③ Artie Lange

3. **Which of these characters does *not* appear in a Bruce Springsteen song?**

    ① Weak-Kneed Willie
    ② Monkey Man
    ③ Magic Rat

4. **How many teams did the National Hockey League begin with?**

    ① 4
    ② 8
    ③ 6

5. **Dick Francis, a former steeplechase jockey, was famous for writing a mystery series based on which sport?**

    ① Polo
    ② Horse racing
    ③ Show jumping

6. **Francis Scott Key penned the words to "The Star Spangled Banner" after witnessing the battle at this famous fort.**

   ① Fort Sumter
   ② Fort George
   ③ Fort McHenry

7. **The elves in the *Lord of the Rings* trilogy speak in a fictional language created by J.R.R. Tolkien called...**

   ① Dothraki
   ② Quenya
   ③ Na'vi

8. **Which of the following sodas was invented first?**

   ① Dr Pepper
   ② Coca-Cola
   ③ Pepsi Cola

9. **A Janka rating determines the hardness of which of the following building materials?**

   ① Wood
   ② Brick
   ③ Glass

10. **The Steadicam was first used in which of these iconic films?**

    ① *Rocky*
    ② *The Shining*
    ③ *Marathon Man*

QUIZ 9

1. **A staple of the New York media scene, *Rolling Stone* magazine was actually founded in this city.**

   ① Los Angeles
   ② San Francisco
   ③ Petaluma

2. **What is another name for the North Star?**

   ① Polaris
   ② Axis Star
   ③ Northpoint

3. **The slogans "War Is Peace," "Freedom Is Slavery," and "Ignorance Is Strength" are from which novel?**

   ① *Catch-22*
   ② *For Whom the Bell Tolls*
   ③ *1984*

4. **Meryl Streep's first Academy Award nomination was for which film?**

   ① *Kramer vs. Kramer*
   ② *The Deer Hunter*
   ③ *Manhattan*

5. **The father of "side whiskers," or sideburns as they are known today, was which of these Civil War generals?**

   ① Robert E. Lee
   ② Ambrose Burnside
   ③ Ulysses S. Grant

6. **Which of the following routes across the United States is the longest?**

① Route 6
② Route 32
③ Route 20

7. **Which country star followed up "Tim McGraw" with "Teardrops on My Guitar"?**

① Faith Hill
② Taylor Swift
③ LeAnn Rimes

8. **Nolan Bushnell, founder of Chuck E. Cheese, is also the founder of which company?**

① Chili's
② Stop & Shop
③ Atari

9. **How many members of the 2004 Red Sox had previously won a World Series?**

① 2
② 4
③ 7

10. **What is the Bank of England also known as?**

① The Queen's Bank
② The Old Lady of Threadneedle Street
③ Newgate's Yard

QUIZ 10

1. **What was the pet's name on _The Flintstones_?**
   - ① Bammer
   - ② Dino
   - ③ Gino

2. **In what year did Steve Wozniak and Steve Jobs build the first Apple personal computer?**
   - ① 1985
   - ② 1976
   - ③ 1981

3. **What famous landmark is in Copenhagen Harbor?**
   - ① A statue of Hans Christian Andersen
   - ② A plaque commemorating Alfred Nobel
   - ③ A statue named _The Little Mermaid_

4. **What are the southern lights called?**
   - ① Aurora Borealis
   - ② Aurora Australis
   - ③ Aurora Arcticus

5. **Curtis Granderson, Jacob deGrom, and Lucas Duda were part of which World Series team?**
   - ① The 2009 Yankees
   - ② The 2015 Mets
   - ③ The 2015 Royals

6. **Who was the first host of TV's *Saturday Night Live*?**

① Chevy Chase
② George Carlin
③ Steve Martin

7. **Why did Georgia O'Keeffe say flowers were better than models?**

① They kept quiet
② They were never late
③ They didn't move

8. **During the filming of *Pirates of the Caribbean*, why did Johnny Depp wear contact lenses?**

① His eyes were too dark
② His eyes were too light
③ As sunglasses

9. **In what year did Serena Williams become a pro tennis player?**

① 1995
② 1999
③ 1989

10. **Which is more abundant in the earth's crust?**

① Uranium
② Gold
③ Silver

QUIZ 11

1. **Traditionally, sumo wrestling is considered which country's national sport?**

    ① China
    ② Taiwan
    ③ Japan

2. **Which man hit a golf ball while he was on the moon?**

    ① Alan Shepard
    ② Pete Conrad
    ③ Neil Armstrong

3. **What does an adult human have an estimated 75 trillion of?**

    ① Blood cells
    ② Cells
    ③ Hairs

4. **Who wrote *The Autobiography of Alice B. Toklas*?**

    ① Eudora Welty
    ② Alice B. Toklas
    ③ Gertrude Stein

5. **Born in Amsterdam, Rembrandt is said to be among the greatest of which painters?**

    ① French
    ② Dutch
    ③ Italian

6. **What company was originally named Blue Ribbon Sports?**

   ① Nike
   ② Spalding
   ③ Converse

7. **What 2013 single by Drake featured an intro by comedian Aziz Ansari that was *not* included on the album?**

   ① "Pound Cake"
   ② "All Me"
   ③ "Started from the Bottom"

8. **Which supervillain was the first to defeat Spider-Man?**

   ① The Green Goblin
   ② Optimus Prime
   ③ Sandman

9. **In which film did Patrick Dempsey make his major film debut?**

   ① *Outbreak*
   ② *Can't Buy Me Love*
   ③ *Heaven Help Us*

10. **Which university featured the Jolly Eight Club?**

    ① Brown
    ② Yale
    ③ Princeton

QUIZ 12

1. **In which movie was Brad Pitt required to have an Irish accent?**

   ① *Twelve Monkeys*
   ② *The Devil's Own*
   ③ *Thelma & Louise*

2. **In "Papa Was a Rolling Stone" what month is mentioned by The Temptations?**

   ① December
   ② January
   ③ September

3. **Which artist became famous for the work *The Birds of America*?**

   ① John James Audubon
   ② Mary Cassatt
   ③ Rube Goldberg

4. **Who started their company marketing the "Maine Hunting Shoe"?**

   ① Eddie Bauer
   ② L.L. Bean
   ③ Abercrombie & Fitch

5. **To which British politician was Princess Diana directly related?**

   ① Sir Winston Churchill
   ② Sir Robert Foster
   ③ Lord Chamberlain

6. **Art Nouveau characteristically has detailed patterns and curving lines plus which design elements?**
   ① Nudes
   ② Geometric shapes
   ③ Leaves, flowers, and vines

7. **Which was the only American sitcom Andy Warhol guest-starred in?**
   ① *Fantasy Island*
   ② *The Love Boat*
   ③ *Three's Company*

8. **Who was U2's "Angel of Harlem" written in honor of?**
   ① John Coltrane
   ② Ella Fitzgerald
   ③ Billie Holiday

9. **Which was Marilyn Monroe's last film?**
   ① *Something's Got to Give*
   ② *Some Like It Hot*
   ③ *River of No Return*

10. **On the New York Stock Exchange, what is a 100-share unit called?**
    ① Regular lot
    ② Even lot
    ③ Round lot

QUIZ 13

1. **What Italian pastry was immortalized in a line from the 1972 film *The Godfather*?**

   ① Biscotti
   ② Cannoli
   ③ Zeppole

2. **Which is one of the largest industries in Iceland?**

   ① Fishing
   ② Growing flowers
   ③ Growing wheat

3. **What was a knight in training called?**

   ① Apprentice
   ② Lord-in-Waiting
   ③ Squire

4. **In 2014 which singer separated from husband Nick Cannon?**

   ① Katy Perry
   ② Mariah Carey
   ③ Lady Gaga

5. **On *The Simpsons*, what is the name of the family restaurant Moe opens?**

   ① Uncle Moe's Family Fooditorium
   ② Moe's Old Fashioned Eatery and Drinkery
   ③ Uncle Moe's Family Feedbag

6. **The value of a diamond is determined by all of these factors except which one?**
   ① Cut
   ② Weight
   ③ Clarity

7. **Which of these rivers is the most southern?**
   ① Amazon
   ② Nile
   ③ Orange

8. **What is the official score of a forfeited Major League Baseball game?**
   ① 1 to 0
   ② 99 to 0
   ③ 9 to 0

9. **Which *Friends* star once appeared on TV's *Cheers*?**
   ① Lisa Kudrow
   ② Matthew Perry
   ③ Jennifer Aniston

10. **On what planet do Anakin and Obi-Wan battle in *Star Wars: Episode III – Revenge of the Sith*?**
    ① Mustafar
    ② Mygeeto
    ③ Hoth

QUIZ 14 (MOVIES)

1. **The famous line "Show me the money" is from which Tom Cruise movie?**
   ① *The Color of Money*
   ② *All the Right Moves*
   ③ *Jerry Maguire*

2. **Which movie is about a young girl in World War II Germany?**
   ① *Out of the Furnace*
   ② *The Book Thief*
   ③ *Prisoners*

3. **Who was the voice of Stinky Pete the Prospector in *Toy Story 2*?**
   ① Kelsey Grammer
   ② Jim Varney
   ③ Don Rickles

4. **In *Madagascar*, what small burrowing animals do the zoo-escaping heroes encounter?**
   ① Lemurs
   ② Rats
   ③ Meerkats

5. **In which 2000 movie did Hugh Jackman play the character Wolverine?**
   ① *Orange County*
   ② *X-Men*
   ③ *A Walk to Remember*

6. **How many Academy Awards did *The Godfather* win?**

    ① 4
    ② 6
    ③ 3

7. **Who starred in *Man of a Thousand Faces*?**

    ① James Cagney
    ② Boris Karloff
    ③ Bela Lugosi

8. **To what grade does Jack Black teach music in *School of Rock*?**

    ① 7th grade
    ② 4th grade
    ③ 9th grade

9. **Which British playwright wrote *Betrayal* and *The French Lieutenant's Woman*?**

    ① Dalton Trumbo
    ② Harold Pinter
    ③ John Osborne

10. **Who directed Gary Cooper in *The Fountainhead*?**

    ① John Ford
    ② Frank Capra
    ③ King Vidor

QUIZ 15

1. **Why was Gary Coleman arrested in January 2010?**
   ① Delinquent property taxes
   ② Child support arrears
   ③ A domestic violence warrant

2. **In the 1976 film *Taxi Driver*, the character Travis Bickle is a veteran of which war?**
   ① Korean War
   ② Vietnam War
   ③ World War II

3. **What is a shark's skeleton made of?**
   ① Cartilage
   ② Marrow
   ③ Bone

4. **Yankee Stadium is built on which famous family's old garden?**
   ① Rockefeller
   ② Astor
   ③ Kennedy

5. **How many years in prison did Nelson Mandela spend before being freed in 1990?**
   ① 20
   ② 40
   ③ 27

6. **Which fashion magazine was first introduced in 1939?**
   ① *Glamour*
   ② *Cosmopolitan*
   ③ *Elle*

7. **Which artist was born first, Leonardo da Vinci or Michelangelo Buonarroti, and by how many years?**
   ① Leonardo, by 40 years
   ② Michelangelo, by 33 years
   ③ Leonardo, by 23 years

8. **What was Christina Yang's minor in college on *Grey's Anatomy*?**
   ① Russian
   ② Psychology
   ③ Mathematics

9. **Who is *not* a character in the novels of Kurt Vonnegut?**
   ① Ignatius J. Reilly
   ② Dwayne Hoover
   ③ Newt Hoenikker

10. **What was the roadie's name in Tom Petty's "Into the Great Wide Open"?**
    ① Johnny
    ② Bart
    ③ Lou

H-QUIZZING TIP

A great way to practice your trivia skills is by doing crossword puzzles.

QUIZ 16

1. **Who founded the Russian city of St. Petersburg?**
   ① Peter the Great
   ② Czar Nicholas II
   ③ Peter Illyich Tchaikovsky

2. **Where is the uvula located in the human body?**
   ① Scrotum
   ② Throat
   ③ Brain

3. **Which fighter was known as "The Louisville Lip"?**
   ① Muhammad Ali
   ② Joey Maxim
   ③ Sugar Ray Leonard

4. **Bluth's Original Frozen Banana Stand is from which TV show?**
   ① *Friends*
   ② *Miami Vice*
   ③ *Arrested Development*

5. **The expression "It is Greek to me" originates from which work?**
   ① *Antony and Cleopatra*
   ② *The Tragedy of Julius Caesar*
   ③ *Othello*

6. **Who sang Paul Simon's "50 Ways to Leave Your Lover" on *SNL*'s 40th anniversary show?**
   ① Miley Cyrus
   ② Lady Gaga
   ③ Jimmy Fallon

7. **In the movie *Grease*, what is Sandy's last name?**
   ① Jensen
   ② Dee
   ③ Olsen

8. **Who was the founder and chairman of America Online Corporation?**
   ① Dennis Ritchie
   ② Steve Case
   ③ William Redington Hewlett

9. **In what year was baseball's World Series first shown on television?**
   ① 1947
   ② 1967
   ③ 1957

10. **In soccer, an "Olympic Goal" is a scored shot taken from which location?**
    ① Penalty arc
    ② Center area
    ③ Corner area

QUIZ 17

1. **How many times did Martina Navratilova win the Ladies' Singles title at Wimbledon?**

   ① 3
   ② 11
   ③ 9

2. **How much skin does each person shed in his or her lifetime?**

   ① 40 pounds
   ② 1,000 pounds
   ③ 1 pound

3. **Who established the UNICEF program?**

   ① United Nations
   ② Microsoft
   ③ American Red Cross

4. **About whom did Gary Oldman say: "It's hard being married to Venus"?**

   ① Kim Basinger
   ② Uma Thurman
   ③ Isabella Rossellini

5. **In *Pulp Fiction*, what was Butch's father's rank while he served in Vietnam?**

   ① Captain
   ② Major
   ③ Sergeant

6. **What does the HP in "HP Sauce" stand for?**

   ① Howard and Poctor
   ② Hot Pepper
   ③ Houses of Parliament

7. **Where did New Zealand's name originate?**

   ① England
   ② Denmark
   ③ An Australian explorer

8. **What instrument measures water vapor in the atmosphere?**

   ① Hygrometer
   ② Spectrometer
   ③ Barometer

9. **In 2012, Bill Belichick was head coach for which NFL team?**

   ① Oakland Raiders
   ② New England Patriots
   ③ Houston Texans

10. **How many members of U2 were actually born in Ireland?**

    ① 3
    ② 4
    ③ 2

QUIZ 18

1. **On *The Sopranos*, what is Tony's favorite TV channel?**

   ① HBO
   ② The History Channel
   ③ ESPN

2. **Of the following, which is a term referring to the melting and cooling of chocolate to make candies?**

   ① Caramelizing
   ② Marbling
   ③ Tempering

3. **The Suez Canal was nationalized by which country?**

   ① Egypt
   ② Jordan
   ③ Israel

4. **When was shortstop Derek Jeter's rookie year?**

   ① 1997
   ② 1994
   ③ 1996

5. **An estuary connects the ocean to a what?**

   ① River
   ② Harbor
   ③ Sea

6. **What did Wassily Kandinsky claim he saw when listening to a good piece of music?**

   ① Letters and numbers
   ② Colors and lines
   ③ Cats and dogs

7. **In which year did the New York Stock Exchange begin?**

   ① 1825
   ② 1805
   ③ 1791

8. **Which was *not* one of the pen names for the 3 Brontë sisters?**

   ① Ganet Bell
   ② Acton Bell
   ③ Curer Bell

9. **What is another name for the big toe?**

   ① Lunate
   ② Hallux
   ③ Pollex

10. **What is forbidden in British Formula 3 racing?**

    ① Traction control
    ② Cruise control
    ③ Ferrous brakes

QUIZ 19

1. **Who sang about "Clouds in my coffee" in the 1970s?**
   - ① Carly Simon
   - ② Carole King
   - ③ Stevie Nicks

2. **Which Spanish artist painted *The Persistence of Memory*?**
   - ① Goya
   - ② Dali
   - ③ Degas

3. **Average hair loss equals how many strands a day?**
   - ① 80
   - ② 40
   - ③ 100

4. **Which revolutionary lived his early life as a fugitive before fleeing to the U.S.?**
   - ① Pancho Villa
   - ② Thomas Jefferson
   - ③ Che Guevara

5. **What was the name of Quint's boat in *Jaws*?**
   - ① *Amity*
   - ② *Orca*
   - ③ *Hooper*

6. **At which age was Tiger Woods first seen on TV playing golf?**

① Age 2
② Age 5
③ Age 16

7. **Which poet wrote "The Red Wheelbarrow"?**

① Wallace Stevens
② Anne Sexton
③ William Carlos Williams

8. **Which is *not* an LP by the supergroup Cream?**

① *Fire Wheels*
② *Disraeli Gears*
③ *Fresh Cream*

9. **Maria Sharapova broke what record on June 21, 2005, at Wimbledon Centre Court?**

① Most consecutive aces
② Loudest grunt
③ Hardest serve

10. **What school does Jake attend in *The Waste Lands* by Stephen King?**

① Markey Academy
② George Washington Elementary
③ Piper

QUIZ 20

1. **Which logo does Shaquille O'Neal have tattooed on his bicep?**

   ① Superman
   ② Spiderman
   ③ Batman

2. **Brine pools in the ocean have an unusually high level of what?**

   ① Sulphur
   ② Salt
   ③ Fish

3. **Which province voted to remain part of Canada in 1995?**

   ① Quebec
   ② Ontario
   ③ Montreal

4. **What does Will Schuester teach on *Glee*?**

   ① Spanish
   ② Wood shop
   ③ English

5. **What did X-rays show exist underneath the final painting of *Mona Lisa*?**

   ① A signature
   ② A poem
   ③ Different versions

6. **In the 1978 movie *Animal House*, what is the mascot of Faber College?**

   ① Lions
   ② Mongols
   ③ Tigers

7. **The July 2007 Concert for Diana was held to raise awareness of what world issue?**

   ① Climate change
   ② World hunger
   ③ AIDS research

8. **According to George Costanza, which city is "...the pesto of cities"?**

   ① New Orleans
   ② San Francisco
   ③ Seattle

9. **"Salto" is a term most commonly used in which sport?**

   ① Gymnastics
   ② Water polo
   ③ Cycling

10. **Which of the following movies was *not* adapted from a James Clavell novel?**

    ① *Shōgun*
    ② *Gunga Din*
    ③ *Tai-Pan*

QUIZ 21

1. **Conan O'Brien earned a degree in American History at which university?**
   ① Brown
   ② Harvard
   ③ Yale

2. **In *District 9*, over which country did the alien craft hover?**
   ① Egypt
   ② Libya
   ③ South Africa

3. **Who became notorious for trying to blow up the English Houses of Parliament?**
   ① Guy Fawkes
   ② Robert Devereux
   ③ Geoffrey Chaucer

4. **What do the words "Magna Carta" mean?**
   ① Magnificent document
   ② Great charter
   ③ Less power

5. **Which author has used the pen name Richard Bachman?**
   ① R. L. Stine
   ② Dean R. Koontz
   ③ Stephen King

6. **Baroque art was a movement encouraged mainly by which religion?**

   ① Catholic
   ② Muslim
   ③ Jewish

7. **Who does William Shatner play on *Boston Legal*?**

   ① Dan Steel
   ② Paul Lewiston
   ③ Denny Crane

8. **What is the name of Rihanna's debut album?**

   ① *Barbados Sunrise*
   ② *Music of the Sun*
   ③ *Umbrella*

9. **In which city in Germany are Audi automobiles mostly produced?**

   ① Wolfsburg
   ② Sindelfingen
   ③ Ingolstadt

10. **Which company invented spray cheese in a can?**

    ① Nabisco
    ② Kraft
    ③ Cracker Barrel

QUIZ 22 (BASKETBALL)

1. **Where was San Antonio Spurs point guard Tony Parker born?**

   ① Bruges, Belgium
   ② Warsaw, Poland
   ③ London, United Kingdom

2. **How many points per game did Markieff Morris average in his rookie season?**

   ① 3.8
   ② 14.9
   ③ 7.4

3. **Who passed Kobe Bryant as the leading scorer in NBA All Star history?**

   ① Chris Paul
   ② LeBron James
   ③ Dwayne Wade

4. **Dikembe Mutombo ended his NBA career at age 42 in 2009 playing for which team?**

   ① Houston Rockets
   ② New York Knicks
   ③ New Jersey Nets

5. **How many double-doubles did Blake Griffin record in his rookie season?**

   ① 48
   ② 63
   ③ 54

6. **What basketball player wore #7 because his father did?**

   ① Michael Jordan
   ② Jake Voskuhl
   ③ Primoz Brezec

7. **Which of the following players did *not* make a single 3-pointer in his rookie season?**

   ① Kenneth Faried
   ② Kawhi Leonard
   ③ Klay Thompson

8. **Who won the 2002–03 NBA Rookie of the Year Award at just 20 years old?**

   ① Josh Childress
   ② Amare Stoudemire
   ③ Carmelo Anthony

9. **David Robinson's #50 was chosen in tribute to which NBA player?**

   ① Ralph Sampson
   ② Larry Bird
   ③ Scottie Pippen

10. **Jan Vesely recorded his first career double-double against which team?**

    ① New York Knicks
    ② Boston Celtics
    ③ Charlotte Bobcats

QUIZ 23

1. **Which arch-villain is finally destroyed at the end of *The Deathly Hallows*?**

    ① Remus Lupin
    ② Sirius Black
    ③ Lord Voldemort

2. **Who released the hit "Boulevard of Broken Dreams" in 2004?**

    ① Green Day
    ② 3 Doors Down
    ③ Nickleback

3. **People with little or no training or formal schooling in art are said to make what type of art?**

    ① Found
    ② Folk
    ③ Mesopotamian

4. **What is the name of the popular Nintendo handheld game system released in 1989?**

    ① 3DO
    ② Super Nintendo
    ③ GameBoy

5. **Who is the Yankee pitcher who wore #35 in 2005?**

    ① Mike Mussina
    ② Al Leiter
    ③ Mariano Rivera

6. **How many squiggles are on top of Hostess CupCakes?**

   ① 9
   ② 5
   ③ 7

7. **With what type of quick drawings did a young Claude Monet begin creating art?**

   ① Caricatures
   ② Silhouettes
   ③ Comic strips

8. ***A Charlie Brown Thanksgiving* marks the first animated appearance of which character?**

   ① Lucy
   ② Marcie
   ③ Pig Pen

9. **Which rapper is *not* featured on Juicy J's 2014 single "Low"?**

   ① Nicki Minaj
   ② Young Thug
   ③ A$AP Ferg

10. **Which animal was part of the Gloria Vanderbilt jeans logo?**

    ① Tiger
    ② Swan
    ③ Goose

H-QUIZZING TIP

In a pinch, try to determine the wrong answer and work from there.

QUIZ 24

1. **Who created the animated series *Futurama*?**
   ① Matt Groening
   ② Larry David
   ③ Seth Green

2. **What word means parts of an image are organized so that one side duplicates or mirrors the other?**
   ① Replica
   ② Symmetry
   ③ Duplicate

3. **Jacqueline "Jackie O" Onassis made popular what style of woman's hat?**
   ① The beret
   ② The pillbox
   ③ The sombrero

4. **Which country has the fewest time zones?**
   ① Mexico
   ② Indonesia
   ③ South Africa

5. **Hines Ward won the 12th season of which game show?**
   ① *Dancing with the Stars*
   ② *Celebrity Apprentice*
   ③ *Survivor*

6. **In Season 5 of *Breaking Bad*, to which country does Walt agree to begin shipping crystal meth?**

   ① Brazil
   ② New York
   ③ Czech Republic

7. **The musical *Rent* is loosely based on what opera?**

   ① *Carmen*
   ② *La Bohème*
   ③ *Faust*

8. **In which movie did Johnny Depp play Gene Watson?**

   ① *Cry-Baby*
   ② *Nick of Time*
   ③ *Dead Man*

9. **Who is the main character in *The Bell Jar*?**

   ① Esther Greenwood
   ② Sylvia Plath
   ③ Lily Bart

10. **How many bones are in a giraffe's neck?**

    ① 36
    ② 82
    ③ 7

QUIZ 25

1. **The only enemy to the orca or killer whale is which of the following predators?**
    ① Great white sharks
    ② Polar bears
    ③ Human beings

2. **Which of the following is a color in the logo of the Cleveland Indians?**
    ① Blue
    ② Teal
    ③ Purple

3. **Lurch was a character on which TV show?**
    ① *The Addams Family*
    ② *The Munsters*
    ③ *Happy Days*

4. **NBA star Kevin Love's uncle, Mike Love, is a founding member of which rock band?**
    ① The Rolling Stones
    ② The Beach Boys
    ③ The Who

5. **Which fear can lead to anxiety attacks and avoidance of high places?**
    ① Microphobia
    ② Anthrophobia
    ③ Acrophobia

6. **Whose album is titled**
   ***The Best of Both Worlds*?**
   ① Van Halen
   ② R.E.M.
   ③ Tool

7. **Georgia O'Keeffe felt that people in the city never had time to really look at what?**
   ① Themselves
   ② Paintings
   ③ Flowers

8. **CNN has used which advertising slogan?**
   ① Keep Going
   ② Fair and Balanced
   ③ Quoted Everywhere

9. **In which year was the first Super Bowl played?**
   ① 1967
   ② 1955
   ③ 1970

10. **In May 2007, an international research group found a gene group possibly responsible for what?**
   ① Alzheimer's disease
   ② Bipolar disorder
   ③ Depression

QUIZ 26

1. **What kind of camp does Andy go to in *Toy Story 2*?**
   ① Cowboy camp
   ② Science camp
   ③ Space camp

2. **What rock group was originally named The Warlocks?**
   ① Pink Floyd
   ② The Grateful Dead
   ③ The Who

3. **When a painting is created in different shades of one color, what is that called?**
   ① Monochrome
   ② Polychrome
   ③ Kodachrome

4. **What classic novel did D. H. Lawrence write in 1928?**
   ① *Cat's Cradle*
   ② *Possession*
   ③ *Lady Chatterley's Lover*

5. **The playing field of the Australian rules football is of what shape?**
   ① Rectangle
   ② Oval
   ③ Square

6. **About how often does Halley's Comet return?**
   ① 76 years
   ② 200 years
   ③ 100 years

7. **At which Grand Slam event did Venus Williams get her first win?**
   ① Wimbledon
   ② Australian Open
   ③ U.S. Open

8. **Which vegetable is *not* in the original V8 Vegetable Juice?**
   ① Lettuce
   ② Watercress
   ③ Broccoli

9. **What was the first product sold by IBM?**
   ① Typewriter
   ② Counting machine
   ③ Cash register

10. **Which filmmaker is an executive producer of the political drama *House of Cards*?**
    ① Steven Spielberg
    ② Alfonso Cuarón
    ③ David Fincher

QUIZ 27

1. **What animated character loves to say "D'oh"?**
    - ① Bart Simpson
    - ② Cartman
    - ③ Homer Simpson

2. **What kind of radiation can be described as infrared?**
    - ① Microwaves
    - ② Heat
    - ③ X-rays

3. **What is the term for a relaxation of tension between countries?**
    - ① Détente
    - ② Filibuster
    - ③ Treaty

4. **What famous chef created the world-renowned Spago's restaurant?**
    - ① Mario Batali
    - ② Wolfgang Puck
    - ③ Julia Child

5. **What is the driest continent on Earth?**
    - ① Asia
    - ② Africa
    - ③ Antarctica

6. **Monica and Big Head are characters in which TV series?**

   ① *Silicon Valley*
   ② *The Alienist*
   ③ *Chicago Hope*

7. **In *Casino*, what is the name of Robert De Niro's character?**

   ① Lester "Two Pairs" Diamond
   ② Sam "Ace" Rothstein
   ③ Remo "Jacks" Gaggi

8. **Which Egyptian king is *not* buried within one of the 3 pyramids at Giza?**

   ① Zoser
   ② Khufu
   ③ Menkaure

9. **Michael Keaton first appeared on television in several episodes of what series?**

   ① *The Andy Griffith Show*
   ② *Mister Rogers' Neighborhood*
   ③ *All in the Family*

10. **Andy Warhol's first notable works were whimsical drawings of which articles of clothing?**

    ① Bowties
    ② Socks
    ③ Shoes

QUIZ 28

1. **From what Shakespeare play is "Good night, sweet prince, And flights of angels sing thee to thy rest"?**

   ① *Othello*
   ② *Henry VIII*
   ③ *Hamlet*

2. **Which of the following is the name of a famous Mexican food company as well as a luthier?**

   ① Goya
   ② Washburn
   ③ Martin

3. **On which soap opera did David Hasselhoff play a doctor?**

   ① *The Young and the Restless*
   ② *As the World Turns*
   ③ *Guiding Light*

4. **Who wrote, "Candy is dandy, but liquor is quicker"?**

   ① Walt Whitman
   ② Ogden Nash
   ③ Thomas Wolfe

5. **What saying is from the hit comedy *Seinfeld*?**

   ① "Did I do that?"
   ② "Hated it."
   ③ "No soup for you!"

6. **What were potato chips first called?**

   ① Saratoga chips
   ② Salted chips
   ③ Summer Spring chips

7. **Which world leader was nicknamed "The Iron Lady"?**

   ① Margaret Thatcher
   ② Jackie Kennedy
   ③ Golda Meir

8. **There is a desk on the U.S. senate floor full of this.**

   ① Money
   ② Pencils
   ③ Candy

9. **This legendary New York jazz club is named after an even more legendary saxophone player?**

   ① Bradley's
   ② Birdland
   ③ Cotton Club

10. **What are the cells that break down bone tissue called?**

   ① Ostomies
   ② Osteoblasts
   ③ Osteoclasts

QUIZ 29

1. **Which stroke in swimming is used almost universally in freestyle races?**
   ① Front crawl
   ② Butterfly
   ③ Breaststroke

2. **Which Rolling Stone bandmember sang background for Carly Simon on "You're So Vain"?**
   ① Keith Richards
   ② Mick Jagger
   ③ Ron Wood

3. **Which country has the largest percent of its land mass on an island?**
   ① Equatorial Guinea
   ② Canada
   ③ Singapore

4. **The term "Altezza lights" refers to what?**
   ① Headlights that give off blue light
   ② Brightly colored brake lights
   ③ Tail lights with LED rings

5. **Which art movement emphasizes the expression of imagination, free of the restraints of reason?**
   ① Surrealism
   ② Realism
   ③ Modernism

6. **In which century was *The Jetsons* set?**

   ① 30th
   ② 21st
   ③ 25th

7. **What number uniform did the 49ers retire for NFL quarterback Joe Montana?**

   ① 11
   ② 16
   ③ 12

8. **What is the process of preparing eggs for Caesar salad dressing called?**

   ① Coddling
   ② Sanitizing
   ③ Chilling

9. **Which political organization did Picasso join in 1944?**

   ① The Nazi Party
   ② The Spanish Republican Resistance
   ③ The French Communist Party

10. **Where is the College Football Hall of Fame located?**

    ① South Bend, Indiana
    ② Ann Arbor, Michigan
    ③ Los Angeles, California

QUIZ 30 (TELEVISION)

1. **How many episodes of *The Voice* were created in its first season?**

    ① 12
    ② 16
    ③ 22

2. **What is the bar featured in *The Drew Carey Show*?**

    ① The Boar's Nest
    ② Jake's
    ③ The Warsaw Tavern

3. **Where did the gang from *Saved by the Bell* hang out?**

    ① The Peach Pit
    ② The Maxx
    ③ The Ballroom

4. **What pro wrestler guested on *Curb Your Enthusiasm*?**

    ① Sven Thorson
    ② Thor Olsen
    ③ Terry Funk

5. **Which was the name of the Bundys' pet dog from *Married with Children*?**

    ① Buck
    ② Skippy
    ③ Lucky

6. **What show features the characters Jet Black and Ein?**

   ① *Cowboy Bebop*
   ② *Aqua Teen Hunger Force*
   ③ *Metalocalypse*

7. **Which actor plays the role of Lincoln Burrows in the TV series *Prison Break*?**

   ① Barry Pepper
   ② Robert Knepper
   ③ Dominic Purcell

8. **Who was originally chosen to play the Hulk on the TV show *The Incredible Hulk*?**

   ① Richard Kiel
   ② Ted Cassidy
   ③ Arnold Schwarzenegger

9. **What show features the characters Skillet and Golden Joe?**

   ① *Lucy, the Daughter of the Devil*
   ② *12 oz. Mouse*
   ③ *Frisky Dingo*

10. **Jami Gertz starred in which CBS TV series?**

    ① *Still Standing*
    ② *Half & Half*
    ③ *One on One*

QUIZ 31

1. **Which country was formerly known as Persia?**
   ① Iran
   ② Iraq
   ③ Egypt

2. **From what TV show did Fall Out Boy take their name?**
   ① *Seinfeld*
   ② *The Simpsons*
   ③ *The X-Files*

3. **Who did Diana Ross play in the film *Lady Sings the Blues*?**
   ① Billie Holiday
   ② Dinah Washington
   ③ Ella Fitzgerald

4. **Which country is totally surrounded by Italy?**
   ① Corsica
   ② San Marino
   ③ Malta

5. **Who painted a view of Phillies Diner at night?**
   ① Grant Wood
   ② Massimo Campigli
   ③ Edward Hopper

6. **Who founded the company Industrial Light & Magic?**

    ① George Lucas
    ② Steven Spielberg
    ③ James Cameron

7. **Which table tennis term refers to the wooden part of the racket?**

    ① Flat
    ② Blade
    ③ Bat

8. **In the film *Mean Girls*, where was Cady Heron raised?**

    ① United States
    ② Australia
    ③ Africa

9. **In Dan Brown's *Angels & Demons*, who is the main antagonist?**

    ① Maximillian Kohler
    ② Robert Langdon
    ③ Carlo Ventresca

10. **Katie Holmes received her first Golden Raspberry Award nomination for which film?**

    ① *Pieces of April*
    ② *Batman Begins*
    ③ *The Giver*

H-QUIZZING TIP

Read as much as possible. Information is power. As one trivia champion suggests, go to the Wikipedia homepage and click on random articles. Do that a few times each day and you'll acquire knowledge you wouldn't have been able to otherwise.

QUIZ 32

1. **What movie is about a rodeo cowboy diag-nosed with AIDS who is given 30 days to live?**
   ① *The Good Thief*
   ② *Prisoners*
   ③ *Dallas Buyers Club*

2. ***Whoa, Nelly!* is the debut album by which artist?**
   ① Nas
   ② Nelly Kim Furtado
   ③ Nelly

3. **Who was the first player to hit home runs from both sides of the plate in one playoff game?**
   ① Bernie Williams
   ② Jorge Posada
   ③ Mickey Mantle

4. **Which characteristic is the most common in Dalmatians?**
   ① Blindness
   ② Deafness
   ③ Extra toes

5. **Which Kurt Vonnegut, Jr. book uses the phrase "so it goes" repeatedly after any character's death?**
   ① *Slaughterhouse-Five*
   ② *Breakfast of Champions*
   ③ *Cat's Cradle*

6. **On what candy wrapper might you find a Native American child shooting an arrow at a star?**
   ① Necco Wafers
   ② Tootsie Roll Pop
   ③ Snickers

7. **Who is the most visually adapted author of all time?**
   ① Agatha Christie
   ② Charles Dickens
   ③ Stephen King

8. **Which Australian defeated World No.1 Rafael Nadal at the 2014 Wimbledon Championships?**
   ① Marinko Matosevic
   ② Samuel Groth
   ③ Nick Kyrgios

9. **How much of an iceberg appears above the water line?**
   ① 1/100
   ② 1/4
   ③ 1/9

10. **Which artist's original canine subjects are named Fay Wray and Man Ray?**
    ① George Segal
    ② William Wegman
    ③ Damien Hirst

QUIZ 33

1. **In which city was Jim Morrison arrested in 1967?**
   ① Los Angeles, California
   ② New Haven, Connecticut
   ③ New York, New York

2. **In real life, from what college did Jerry Seinfeld graduate?**
   ① New York University
   ② Cornell
   ③ Queens College

3. **What year did Spain cede Florida to the United States?**
   ① 1819
   ② 1902
   ③ 1860

4. **According to this cliché, "actions speak louder than..."**
   ① Pictures
   ② Words
   ③ Screams

5. **What was the most important celestial object to the Aztecs?**
   ① The moon
   ② Venus
   ③ The sun

6. **Tim Duncan is nicknamed "Merlin" due to his interest in what hobby?**

   ① Dungeons and Dragons
   ② The occult
   ③ Amateur magic tricks

7. **Which national park is directly west of the Painted Desert?**

   ① Grand Canyon
   ② Petrified Forest
   ③ Carlsbad Caverns

8. **In which city is the price of gold "fixed" daily?**

   ① London
   ② New York
   ③ Paris

9. **Tea leaves rolled into small round pellets are called what?**

   ① Darjeeling
   ② Irish Breakfast
   ③ Gunpowder tea

10. **What is the name of the gossip columnist in the *Batman* films?**

    ① Gossip Gerty
    ② Showbiz Sheena
    ③ Fannie Landers

QUIZ 34

1. **In 2014, Justin Bieber was arrested for DUI and drag racing in which city?**

    ① Miami
    ② New York
    ③ St. Louis

2. **Anne Hathaway starred as which character in the 2014 sci-fi film *Interstellar*?**

    ① Lois Cooper
    ② Murphy "Murph" Cooper
    ③ Dr. Amelia Brand

3. **Which fruit contains more Vitamin C than oranges?**

    ① Mandarin
    ② Kiwi
    ③ Pineapple

4. **Which African country has a capital named for a U.S. president?**

    ① Sierra Leone
    ② Liberia
    ③ Gambia

5. **Ebbets Field was once home to which team?**

    ① Brooklyn Dodgers
    ② Boston Braves
    ③ New York Yankees

6. **In which ocean would one find the Sargasso Sea?**
   ① Atlantic
   ② Pacific
   ③ Indian

7. **What is the first name of the *South Park* mayor?**
   ① Nancy
   ② Mary
   ③ Teri

8. **Who was the first female singer enshrined in the Rock & Roll Hall of Fame?**
   ① Aretha Franklin
   ② Dusty Springfield
   ③ Janis Joplin

9. **Which manga artist was the world's bestselling female comic artist in 2008?**
   ① Clamp
   ② Yuu Watase
   ③ Rumiko Takahashi

10. **What was the original name of Epcot Center's "Innovations"?**
    ① Communicore
    ② Connections
    ③ Centercom

QUIZ 35

1. **Who designed the modern woman's suit, comprised of a cinched blazer and fitted, knee-length skirt?**
   ① Ralph Lauren
   ② Yves Saint Laurent
   ③ Coco Chanel

2. **Which style of art from the 19th century featured bold and dramatic emotions?**
   ① Realism
   ② Romanticism
   ③ Pop Art

3. **What is golfer Jack Nicklaus' nickname?**
   ① The Golden Bear
   ② The Golden Hat
   ③ Goldeneye

4. **Which mythical creature was supposedly born from the egg of a rooster?**
   ① Minotaur
   ② Basilisk
   ③ Dragon

5. **What one ingredient must a fish or poultry dish have to be called "Veronique"?**
   ① Mayonnaise
   ② Eggs
   ③ Grapes

6. **What was the first Disney animated classic to be released on video?**

    ① *Snow White and the Seven Dwarfs*
    ② *Dumbo*
    ③ *Fantasia*

7. **Jarvis Cocker is the singer of what Brit-Pop band?**

    ① Oasis
    ② Blur
    ③ Pulp

8. **Whitney Houston sang the national anthem at which Super Bowl?**

    ① Super Bowl 23, 1988–89 Season
    ② Super Bowl 20, 1985–86 Season
    ③ Super Bowl 25, 1990–91 Season

9. **Where in the world is a monument to a bug located?**

    ① Enterprise, Alabama
    ② Atlanta, Georgia
    ③ Des Moines, Iowa

10. **In what year did Microsoft ship the first Windows programs?**

    ① 1990
    ② 1983
    ③ 1989

QUIZ 36

1. **On *Sex and the City*, who has an on-and-off relationship with a mysterious man they call Mr. Big?**
   ① Dana Scully
   ② Miranda Hobbes
   ③ Carrie Bradshaw

2. **At the age of 21, Kate Hudson married the lead singer of which band?**
   ① Counting Crows
   ② The Black Crowes
   ③ Oasis

3. **What is the name of the sauce that traditionally accompanies souvlaki?**
   ① Tzatziki
   ② Taratoor
   ③ Chocolate

4. **Where was the first Christmas card printed?**
   ① England
   ② Canada
   ③ USA

5. **Who did the Marlins beat to win their first-ever World Series title?**
   ① Boston Red Sox
   ② Cleveland Indians
   ③ New York Yankees

6. **What is a male camel known as?**
   ① Bull
   ② Buck
   ③ Stag

7. **Who wrote *The Tin Drum* where the main character can shatter glass with a scream?**
   ① Franz Kafka
   ② Hermann Hesse
   ③ Günter Grass

8. **What candy bar was originally named "Kandy Kake"?**
   ① Snickers
   ② Baby Ruth
   ③ Heath bar

9. **Which figure skater wore a Vera Wang outfit in the 1994 Olympics?**
   ① Michelle Kwan
   ② Tonya Harding
   ③ Nancy Kerrigan

10. **In the movie *Iron Man*, Tony Stark is kidnapped when he travels to what country?**
    ① Afghanistan
    ② Bolivia
    ③ Russia

QUIZ 37

1. **What does the Russian newspaper's name *Pravda* mean in English?**
   ① Truth
   ② Knowledge
   ③ Official

2. **What did the Father, Son, and Holy Ghost do in the song "American Pie"?**
   ① Introduced him to Will Rogers and Wiley Post
   ② Killed the man that they loved most
   ③ Caught the last train for the coast

3. **Which writer killed his wife while trying to shoot a glass off her head?**
   ① William S. Burroughs
   ② Norman Mailer
   ③ Jack Kerouac

4. **Which constellation represents a hunter with weapons?**
   ① Andromeda
   ② Orion
   ③ Hercules

5. **In 2013, who said if he had a son he'd think twice about letting him play football?**
   ① Mike Bloomberg
   ② Barak Obama
   ③ Bryant Gumbel

6. **What is the name of the main character played by Logan Lerman in *The Perks of Being a Wallflower*?**
   ① Charlie
   ② Patrick
   ③ Brad

7. **How many points are there on Lisa's head on *The Simpsons*?**
   ① 6
   ② 4
   ③ 8

8. **Which portrait artist switched to painting seated in a forklift after an injury?**
   ① Alice Neel
   ② Chuck Close
   ③ Duane Hanson

9. **Who created the Cabbage Patch Kids?**
   ① Andrew McNally
   ② Mr. Cabbage
   ③ Xavier Roberts

10. **What is the capital of Pitcairn Island?**
    ① Adamstown
    ② Pitcairn
    ③ Fletcher

QUIZ 38 (POP MUSIC)

1. **Gwen Stefani's song "Harajuku Girls" is an ode to what?**

    ① Japanese all girl bands
    ② Japanese music scene
    ③ Japanese pop culture

2. **Who cowrote Kelly Clarkson's single "Miss Independent"?**

    ① Beyoncé
    ② Christina Aguilera
    ③ Avril Lavigne

3. **Who wrote the 2005 hit song "Daughters"?**

    ① John Mayer
    ② Weezer
    ③ Maroon 5

4. **What instrument does Boyd Tinsley play in the Dave Matthews Band?**

    ① Violin
    ② Drums
    ③ Bass

5. **Which singer's *Christmas* album went 7x Platinum in Canada, surpassing his 2009 album *Crazy Love*?**

    ① Bryan Adams
    ② Jacob Hoggard
    ③ Michael Bublé

6. **Who wrote "Some Beach" recorded by Blake Shelton?**

   ① John Rich
   ② Paul Overstreet
   ③ Faith Hill

7. **Which of the following artists received writer credit on Adam Lambert's single "Whataya Want from Me"?**

   ① Pink
   ② Alicia Keys
   ③ Adam Lambert

8. **Which artist released an album titled *Survivor*?**

   ① Aaliyah
   ② Jagged Edge
   ③ Alanis Morissette

9. **Which single by Bruno Mars spent 22 weeks in the *Billboard* Top 10 in 2010?**

   ① "Grenade"
   ② "The Lazy Song"
   ③ "Just the Way You Are"

10. **The music video for which Coldplay track pays tribute to silent films and stars Chinese actress Zhang Ziyi?**

    ① "Midnight"
    ② "Magic"
    ③ "A Sky Full of Stars"

QUIZ 39 (HIP HOP)

1. **What member of the rap group Wu-Tang Clan was known as the Chef?**

   ① Method Man
   ② RZA
   ③ Raekwon

2. **Which rap artist appears in Britney Spears' music video "Outrageous"?**

   ① Snoop Dogg
   ② Busta Rhymes
   ③ Vanilla Ice

3. **What "alter ego" of Nicki Minaj helped name her second studio album?**

   ① Roman Zolanski
   ② Nicki Teresa
   ③ Rosa

4. **Which seminal 1990 rap hit is sampled in Big Sean's 2012 single "Dance"?**

   ① "Ice, Ice Baby"
   ② "Can't Touch This"
   ③ "My Adidas"

5. **Which member of the Beastie Boys sadly passed away in 2012?**

   ① Mike "Mike D" Diamond
   ② Adam "Ad-Rock" Horovitz
   ③ Adam "MCA" Yauch

6. **The music video for which Drake song won Best Hip Hop Video at the 2014 BET Hip Hop Awards?**

① "Started from the Bottom"
② "Worst Behavior"
③ "Hold On, We're Going Home"

7. **Which single from Pusha T's debut studio album *My Name Is My Name* features Kendrick Lamar?**

① "Nosetalgia"
② "Let Me Love You"
③ "Numbers on the Boards"

8. **The remix of what 2014 single by G-Eazy features an additional verse by Rick Ross?**

① "Far Alone"
② "Let's Get Lost"
③ "I Mean It"

9. **The 2014 BET Hip Hop Award for Lyricist of the Year went to which rapper?**

① Nicki Minaj
② Kendrick Lamar
③ Drake

10. **The 2013 album *Trap Lord* is the debut studio album by which A$AP Mob member?**

① A$AP Ferg
② A$AP Rocky
③ A$AP Nast

H-QUIZZING TIP

Practice your trivia skills by playing trivia games. Go online and play Sporcle. Attend a trivia night and compete against other people in a live setting. The more you play, the better you get. Like any sport, practice is essential for getting better.

QUIZ 40 (STAR WARS)

1. **In _Star Wars: Episode IV - A New Hope_, who was Jabba's main rival?**

   ① Lady Valarian
   ② The Emperor
   ③ Han Solo

2. **In the movie _Star Wars: Episode IV - A New Hope_, what race was Greedo?**

   ① Correlian
   ② Mon Calamari
   ③ Rodian

3. **In _Star Wars: Episode IV - A New Hope_, who was the aide to Grand Moff Tarkin?**

   ① Boba Fett
   ② Chief Bast
   ③ Commander Praji

4. **An accident ended George Lucas' ambition to be what?**

   ① Professional race car driver
   ② Park ranger
   ③ Ski instructor

5. **Which species is Bossk a member of in _Star Wars: Episode IV - A New Hope_?**

   ① Gand
   ② Ithorian
   ③ Trandoshan

6. In *Star Wars*, in what cell block was Princess Leia held?

    ① Aa-23
    ② H
    ③ 309

7. Which Akira Kurosawa movie provided George Lucas with the inspiration for *Star Wars*?

    ① *Ikiru*
    ② *The Hidden Fortress*
    ③ *Yojimbo*

8. Which *Star Wars* film was *not* nominated for a Best Visual Effects Oscar?

    ① *Episode V - The Empire Strikes Back*
    ② *Episode I - The Phantom Menace*
    ③ *Episode III - Revenge of the Sith*

9. On what planet do Anakin and Obi-Wan battle in *Star Wars: Episode III – Revenge of the Sith*?

    ① Mustafar
    ② Mygeeto
    ③ Hoth

10. In *Star Wars: Episode III – Revenge of the Sith*, what species is Jedi Master Shaak Ti?

    ① Human
    ② Togruta
    ③ Hutt

QUIZ 41 (BOXING)

1. **To which boxer did Sugar Ray Robinson lose his last professional fight?**
   ① Joey Archer
   ② Joey Giardello
   ③ Paul Pender

2. **Which boxer split a pair of fights against Johnathan Barros in 2011?**
   ① Jason Litzau
   ② Steve Molitor
   ③ Celestino Caballero

3. **Which fighter was knocked out by Nonito Donaire in their 2011 bantamweight fight?**
   ① Martin Castillo
   ② Fernando Montiel
   ③ Vic Darchinyan

4. **Which fighter was forced to retire after 8 rounds against Felix Sturm in 2012?**
   ① Ronald Hearns
   ② Khoren Gevor
   ③ Sebastian Zbik

5. **Which fighter scored a brutal knockout win over Roy Jones, Jr. in 2011?**
   ① Denis Lebedev
   ② Shawn Terry Cox
   ③ Marco Huck

6. **In which round did Floyd Mayweather Jr. knock out Victor Ortiz in their 2011 duel?**

① 2nd
② 8th
③ 4th

7. **Which country won 3 gold medals at the 2010 Summer Youth Olympics?**

① Cuba
② Ireland
③ Australia

8. **Which tagline was used for a 2011 fight between Sergio Martinez and Sergiy Dzinziruk?**

① Fire and Ice
② The Threat Is Real
③ Showdown

9. **In April of 2012, Koki Kameda won his fight against Nouldy Manakane in which Japanese city?**

① Yokohama
② Hiroshima
③ Tokyo

10. **In what country was boxer Urbano Antillón born?**

① Nicaragua
② Spain
③ Mexico

QUIZ 42 (BASEBALL)

1. **What position did Victor Martinez originally play?**

   ① First base
   ② Third base
   ③ Catcher

2. **How many games did the Mets and Yankees play in the 2000 World Series?**

   ① 5
   ② 4
   ③ 7

3. **In 1994, Ken Griffey Jr. became only the thirteenth player to do what?**

   ① Drive in 175 runs
   ② Steal 40 bases/hit 40 HR
   ③ Hit 30 HR before the All-Star Break

4. **Who else did the Minnesota Twins acquire in the trade that brought them Joe Nathan?**

   ① Francisco Liriano
   ② Justin Morneau
   ③ Johan Santana

5. **For how many seasons was Lou Piniella the manager of the Seattle Mariners?**

   ① 8
   ② 9
   ③ 10

6. **How did the New York Mets acquire Tom Seaver?**
   - ① By trade
   - ② Lottery
   - ③ Free agency

7. **Which player hit the most home runs in the 1960 World Series?**
   - ① Bill Mazeroski
   - ② Roger Maris
   - ③ Mickey Mantle

8. **Who finished runner-up to Vladimir Guerrero in the 2004 American League MVP voting?**
   - ① Gary Sheffield
   - ② Manny Ramirez
   - ③ David Ortiz

9. **Who was the first Major Leaguer to reach 3,000 hits in a career?**
   - ① Eddie Collins
   - ② Cap Anson
   - ③ Honus Wagner

10. **Who won the most Gold Gloves as a San Francisco Giant in the 1990s?**
    - ① Barry Bonds
    - ② J. T. Snow
    - ③ Will Clark

QUIZ 43 (FOOTBALL)

1. **The Cowboys have their own Hall of Fame; what is it called?**

    ① Texas Heroes
    ② Cowboy Honor Ranch
    ③ Ring of Honor

2. **What former NFL star invented "The Mile High Salute"?**

    ① Terrell Davis
    ② Terry Bradshaw
    ③ John Elway

3. **During which game did the replacement referees of 2012 commit the biggest blunder of their short-lived careers?**

    ① The Chargers and the Raiders
    ② The Ravens and the Chiefs
    ③ The Packers and the Seahawks

4. **NFL Hall of Fame quarterback Dan Fouts played for which college?**

    ① Stanford
    ② Oregon
    ③ Grambling

5. **Who was the first person to win 5 Super Bowl rings as a player?**

    ① Charles Haley
    ② Joe Montana
    ③ Roger Staubach

6. **Which of these players did *not* win multiple Super Bowl MVP Awards?**

   ① Terry Bradshaw
   ② Troy Aikman
   ③ Bart Starr

7. **Which of the following running backs has won the NFL's regular season MVP Award?**

   ① Barry Sanders
   ② Eric Dickerson
   ③ Marcus Allen

8. **In what round of the draft was Boomer Esiason picked by the Cincinnati Bengals?**

   ① 3rd round
   ② 1st round
   ③ 2nd round

9. **Who scored the first Super Bowl touchdown in Tennessee Titans history?**

   ① Steve McNair
   ② Eddie George
   ③ Frank Wycheck

10. **What is the name of the Seahawks' cheerleaders?**

    ① Hawk Girls
    ② Sea Gals
    ③ Seahawk Cheerleaders

QUIZ 44 (GOLF)

1. **How many LPGA Tour events did Yani Tseng win in 2011?**
   ① 7
   ② 3
   ③ 9

2. **In what year was golf ball weight and size standardized by the USGA?**
   ① 1908
   ② 1960
   ③ 1932

3. **Which golf course was chosen to host the 2012 U.S. Open?**
   ① Olympic Club
   ② Oakmont
   ③ Pebble Beach

4. **Which golfer is nicknamed "El Niño"?**
   ① Sergio Garcia
   ② Johnny Miller
   ③ Tom Watson

5. **Which golfer won his first World Golf Championship event at the 2014 WGC-Bridgestone Invitational?**
   ① Sergio Garcia
   ② Rory McIlroy
   ③ Keegan Bradley

6. **Which of the following awards did Matt Kuchar *not* win in 2010?**

① Jack Nicklaus Trophy
② Byron Nelson Award
③ Arnold Palmer Award

7. **Which of the following Champions Tour events did Fred Couples win in 2011?**

① Cap Cana Championship
② Toshiba Classic
③ AT&T Championship

8. **In 2012, the PGA announced that the 2014 PGA season would officially begin in which month of 2013?**

① December
② October
③ September

9. **What is Jack Nicklaus' favorite course?**

① Pebble Beach
② Augusta National
③ St. Andrews

10. **What did Tiger Woods win to overtake Vijay Singh atop the 2005 world golf rankings?**

① The Masters
② Ford Championship
③ PGA Championship

QUIZ 45 (HOCKEY)

1. **Who led the NHL in scoring during the 2011–12 season?**
   ① Claude Giroux
   ② Ilya Kovalchuk
   ③ Evgeni Malkin

2. **Which NHL franchise won its sixth Stanley Cup in 2011?**
   ① New York Rangers
   ② Boston Bruins
   ③ Chicago Blackhawks

3. **Which of these teams ended up the 2014–15 season with more points?**
   ① Pittsburgh Penguins
   ② Los Angeles Kings
   ③ Columbus Blue Jackets

4. **In 2012, which goaltender became the first in NHL history to start his career with seven 30-win seasons?**
   ① Jean-Sébastien Giguére
   ② Cam Ward
   ③ Henrik Lundqvist

5. **Who led the NHL with 56 goals to win the Hart Trophy as League MVP in 2009?**
   ① Alexander Ovechkin
   ② Jonathan Toews
   ③ Evgeni Malkin

6. **In what category did Saku Koivu lead all players at the 2006 Turin Olympics?**
   ① Assists
   ② Goals
   ③ Shots on goal

7. **Who did the Dallas Stars give up to get Kari Lehtonen?**
   ① Riley Nash
   ② Ivan Vishnevskiy
   ③ Jeff Halpern

8. **How many total games did the Los Angeles Kings lose during the 2011–12 Stanley Cup playoffs?**
   ① 4
   ② 5
   ③ 6

9. **The first 12 picks of the 2011 NHL entry draft were natives of either Canada or which country?**
   ① The United States
   ② Sweden
   ③ Czech Republic

10. **The 2010–11 NHL season was the first time that this number of penalty shot goals were scored in one night?**
    ① 3
    ② 5
    ③ 4

H-QUIZZING TIP

Come with a clear head. Given that each game lasts about 15 or 20 minutes, you should treat it as a break, a chance to shake off stress or have some fun. The less distracted you are, the better you'll perform.

QUIZ 46

1. **In which country is the 1979 film *Mad Max* set?**
   ① Australia
   ② Mexico
   ③ United States

2. **Which former California First Lady was offered $15 million in 2011 to write a tell-all memoir?**
   ① Nancy Reagan
   ② Maria Shriver
   ③ Michelle Obama

3. **Which Led Zeppelin album cover features the *Hindenburg* exploding?**
   ① *Led Zeppelin III*
   ② *Physical Graffiti*
   ③ *Led Zeppelin I*

4. **Peter Paul Rubens' paintings featured women who differed from other painters' subjects in what way?**
   ① They were well rounded
   ② They were asleep
   ③ They were clothed

5. **What is the major ingredient in the British foodstuff called "Marmite"?**
   ① Pork drippings
   ② Bean curd
   ③ Yeast extract

6. **Which American realist authored the short story "The Beast in the Jungle"?**

① Henry James
② Stephen Crane
③ Mark Twain

7. **Which tiny moon orbiting the asteroid Ida was discovered in 1994?**

① Eros
② Dactyl
③ Icarus

8. **What is the minimum distance considered to be a marathon swim?**

① 10 kilometers
② 8 kilometers
③ 5 kilometers

9. **What manufacturer introduced Pringles potato chips in 1969?**

① Procter & Gamble
② Better Made Snack Foods
③ Frito-Lay

10. **What record label did the head of Phat Farm clothing company Russell Simmons cofound?**

① Bad Boy Records
② Def Jam Recordings
③ Disturbing Tha Peace

QUIZ 47

1. **In ancient Athens, what was the systematic study of oratory called?**
   ① Grammar
   ② Rhetoric
   ③ Creative writing

2. **The color of light is determined by what?**
   ① Its wavelength
   ② Atmospheric conditions
   ③ Intensity of the power source

3. **All of following are NFL siblings except which pair?**
   ① Bruce and Clay Matthews
   ② Tiki and Rondé Barber
   ③ Peyton and Archie Manning

4. **Who wrote the book *The Count of Monte Cristo*?**
   ① William Shakespeare
   ② Alexandre Dumas
   ③ Douglas Adams

5. **What is the capital city of Martinique, the West Indies' island that is about 40 miles long and 12 miles wide?**
   ① Fort-de-France
   ② Sainte-Marie
   ③ Schœlcher

6. **What is an alternative name for the *Mona Lisa*?**

① *Mother*
② *Un Domingo*
③ *La Gioconda*

7. **What is the name of the BBC show on which the TV show *Dancing with the Stars* is based?**

① *Dance the Night Away*
② *Strictly Come Dancing*
③ *Stars Come Dancing*

8. **What was Martin Scorsese's first feature film?**

① *Taxi Driver*
② *Who's That Knocking at My Door?*
③ *Mean Streets*

9. **Which song was the Foo Fighters' first #1 hit in the United States?**

① "Learn to Fly"
② "Monkey Wrench"
③ "My Hero"

10. **The Tour de France bicycle race was first run in what year?**

① 1979
② 1963
③ 1903

QUIZ 48

1. **Which member of the Marvel Universe is called the Prince of Power?**
   ① Hercules
   ② Colossus
   ③ Wonder Man

2. **What Major League team played their home games at Crosley Field?**
   ① Cincinnati Reds
   ② Chicago Cubs
   ③ Seattle Pilots

3. **What was at the heart of a 2011 lawsuit that involved Tobey Maguire?**
   ① Parking tickets
   ② An illegal poker ring
   ③ Contract negotiations

4. **Claude Monet's Rouen Cathedral series showed architectural depth by laying paint onto canvas how?**
   ① Quickly
   ② Thinly
   ③ Thickly

5. **Most terms that help to identify vulcanological events come from which language?**
   ① Hawaiian
   ② Latin
   ③ Greek

6. **What Police hit did Sting and Gwen Stefani sing at halftime at the 2003 Super Bowl?**

① "King of Pain"
② "Message in a Bottle"
③ "Every Breath You Take"

7. **Who in 2013 had a hit titled "I Will Wait"?**

① Miley Cyrus
② Lana Del Rey & Cedric Gervais
③ Mumford & Sons

8. **How many times does Chuck encounter a whale while adrift in the movie *Cast Away*?**

① 3
② 7
③ 5

9. **Which HTML tag is used to create an image map?**

① Imagemap="#Mapname"
② Map="#Mapname"
③ Usemap="#Mapname"

10. **When she appeared in the CBS network's first color commercial, what was Betty Crocker baking?**

① Apple Brown Betty
② Mystery Fruitcake
③ Chocolate Chip cookies

QUIZ 49

1. **In which movie did Nicolas Cage make his screen debut?**

   ① *Birdy*
   ② *Fast Times at Ridgemont High*
   ③ *Valley Girl*

2. **Which number is the title of a 2011 album by Adele?**

   ① 21
   ② 4
   ③ 13

3. **Which sea lies at one end of the Great Wall of China?**

   ① The Sea of China
   ② The Yellow Sea
   ③ The White Sea

4. **What was the family name of Mary, Queen of Scots?**

   ① Stuart
   ② Windsor
   ③ Macloud

5. **What was the name of Lloyd's and Harry's bird in *Dumb and Dumber*?**

   ① Pauly
   ② Pokey
   ③ Petey

6. **Which country always enters first during the opening ceremonies of the Olympics?**
   ① The host country
   ② United States
   ③ Greece

7. **Karst topography is most likely to occur in which type of rock?**
   ① Limestone
   ② Slate
   ③ Sandstone

8. **Which author has written the *Sweet Valley High* series of books?**
   ① Valerie Tripp
   ② Francine Pascal
   ③ Judy Blume

9. **Popped kernels of popcorn come in 2 shapes, butterfly and what?**
   ① Mushroom
   ② Cauliflower
   ③ Spider

10. **Who was the founder of the pathetic art movement?**
   ① Mike Kelley
   ② Cady Noland
   ③ Christo

QUIZ 50

1. **The creation of art with stones, leaves, and dirt is called what?**

    ① Art Nouveau
    ② Earth art
    ③ Etruscan art

2. **Which actress portrayed reporter Zoe Barnes in the political drama TV series *House of Cards*?**

    ① Kate Mara
    ② Robin Wright
    ③ Rooney Mara

3. **What song got Elvis Costello banned from *Saturday Night Live* for 12 years?**

    ① "Living in Paradise"
    ② "Radio Radio"
    ③ "Alison"

4. **Situated on the southern slopes of the Pyrenees Mountains, Andorra boasts which capital city?**

    ① Andorra la Vella
    ② Les Escales
    ③ Encamp

5. **Which king had a pie delivered to him by Little Jack Horner?**

    ① King Henry VI
    ② King Henry V
    ③ King Henry VIII

6. **In what modern-day country did the dog called the Rhodesian Ridgeback originate?**
   ① South Africa
   ② India
   ③ South Arabia

7. **Which baseball player was known as the "Space Man"?**
   ① Bob Stanley
   ② Bill Lee
   ③ Derek Lower

8. **Who was the chairman of the President's Council on Physical Fitness and Sports in 2004?**
   ① Hulk Hogan, former wrestler
   ② Michael Jordan, former NBA star
   ③ Lynn Swann, former Pittsburgh Steeler

9. **What blues musician was the bass player for Otis Day and the Knights in *Animal House*?**
   ① Buddy Guy
   ② Robert Cray
   ③ John Lee Hooker

10. **What was the setting for the TV sitcom *Good Times*?**
   ① Chicago
   ② New York
   ③ Cleveland

QUIZ 51

1. **What is the name of a football coach in _Friday Night Lights_?**

   ① Smash Williams
   ② Ray Romano
   ③ Eric Taylor

2. **One of Michelangelo's earliest sculptures was a Madonna sitting on what?**

   ① Footstool
   ② Stairs
   ③ Tree branch

3. **Which member of the Wu-Tang Clan is referred to as "The Abbot"?**

   ① Raekwon
   ② RZA
   ③ Method Man

4. **With which vegetable are Norwegian lefse made?**

   ① Potatoes
   ② Zucchini
   ③ Cabbage

5. **How long is a jiffy?**

   ① 1 second
   ② 1/10 minute
   ③ 1/100th of a second

6. **In 2012 what was the name of the stadium the Giants and the Jets shared?**

   ① Raymond James Stadium
   ② MetLife Stadium
   ③ Heinz Field

7. **What show features the characters Killface and The X-tacles?**

   ① *Frisky Dingo*
   ② *The Boondocks*
   ③ *Cowboy Bebop*

8. **What was the first award show that Ellen DeGeneres hosted?**

   ① Oscars
   ② Grammys
   ③ Razzies

9. **What demonic entity is the primary villain of *Green Lantern*?**

   ① Deimos
   ② Parallax
   ③ Genocide

10. **How old was Olympic star Shaun White at the 2018 Winter Olympics?**

    ① 28
    ② 20
    ③ 31

QUIZ 52

1. **In table tennis, how high above the playing surface should the top of the net be?**
   ① 1 inch
   ② 6 inches
   ③ 12 inches

2. **When did *The Mary Tyler Moore Show* go off the air?**
   ① 1993
   ② 1997
   ③ 1977

3. **How does the end of the world start according to R.E.M.?**
   ① With an earthquake
   ② With a tidal wave
   ③ With an explosion

4. **Georgia O'Keeffe was married to which famous photographer?**
   ① Alfred Eisenstaedt
   ② Alfred Stieglitz
   ③ Ansel Adams

5. **Who became Czar of Russia at age 10, co-ruling with his half-brother Ivan V?**
   ① Peter I
   ② Ivan the Terrible
   ③ Michael Romanov

6. **Which of Rihanna's songs shares its name with a William Shakespeare play?**

   ① "Macbeth"
   ② "King Lear"
   ③ "Romeo and Juliet"

7. **Which of the following is *not* a type of white blood cell?**

   ① Eosinophile
   ② Erythrophile
   ③ Neutrophile

8. **Which ballplayer was given the nickname "El Titan de Bronze" by Fidel Castro?**

   ① Raul Mondesi
   ② José Contreras
   ③ Luis Tiant

9. **In which district of the United Kingdom is Scaffel Pike, England's highest peak, found?**

   ① The Peak District
   ② Merseyside
   ③ The Lake District

10. **What is Rob Reiner's character name in *This Is Spinal Tap*?**

    ① Marty Dibergi
    ② Tom Winstein
    ③ John Winstein

QUIZ 53

1. **What *Saturday Night Live* stars played Wayne and Garth?**

    ① Phil Hartman and Kevin Nealon
    ② Rob Schneider and David Spade
    ③ Mike Meyers and Dana Carvey

2. **When tea leaves unfold as they steep it is sometimes called what?**

    ① The agony of the leaves
    ② Autumnal steeping
    ③ Scrolling

3. **What precious gem was found to be plentiful in South Africa in the 1860s?**

    ① Emerald
    ② Diamond
    ③ Sapphire

4. **What is the penalty in the NFL for an illegal substitution?**

    ① 10-yard penalty
    ② 5-yard penalty
    ③ 15-yard penalty

5. **Which group inducted into the Rock & Roll Hall of Fame in 2012 consists of Mike D, MCA, and Ad Rock?**

    ① Run-D.M.C.
    ② Cypress Hill
    ③ The Beastie Boys

6. **What breed of dog was Eddie on *Frasier*?**

    ① Jack Russell Terrier
    ② Cocker Spaniel
    ③ Beagle

7. **What tea company was bought by Starbucks in 1999?**

    ① Lipton
    ② Tazo
    ③ Celestial Seasonings

8. **Who won Best Supporting Actress at the 89th Academy Awards held in February 2017?**

    ① Viola Davis
    ② Zoe Saldana
    ③ Michelle Williams

9. **In 2005, what did Bill Gates receive over 4,000,000 times a day?**

    ① Spam email
    ② Phone calls
    ③ Copies of new software

10. **Where was the Fauvism art movement first introduced?**

    ① Germany
    ② Italy
    ③ France

QUIZ 54

1. **What TV show used the back room of the Bada Bing! club to hang out?**

   ① *Entourage*
   ② *The Sopranos*
   ③ *Starsky & Hutch*

2. **Which band wanted you to "Bang Your Head"?**

   ① Quiet Riot
   ② Mötley Crüe
   ③ Judas Priest

3. **Which type of art was dominant in Germany during the early 1900s?**

   ① Cubism
   ② Expressionism
   ③ The Harlem Renaissance

4. **You can find the Escorial Palace at which location?**

   ① Spain
   ② Panama
   ③ China

5. **Which star, other than the sun, is closest to Earth?**

   ① Betelgeuse
   ② Centauri B
   ③ Alpha Centauri C

6. **The title of Aldous Huxley's *Brave New World* comes from which Shakespearean play?**

① *Romeo and Juliet*
② *Richard III*
③ *The Tempest*

7. **How old was Kobe Bryant when he was drafted into the NBA?**

① 17
② 20
③ 18

8. **What actor plays R. L. Stine in the movie *Goosebumps*?**

① Dylan McDermott
② Jack Black
③ James Franco

9. **What was the first website to feature a banner advertisement?**

① Hotwired
② Yahoo!
③ Amazon

10. **"Daffy" is a term most commonly used in which sport?**

① Wrestling
② Skiing
③ Curling

QUIZ 55

1. **Why is the face-first luge race called "Skeleton?"**

   ① Participants are rail thin
   ② The sport is really scary
   ③ The first sled resembled a skeleton

2. **How much blood does the average adult have in his body?**

   ① 25 pints
   ② 120 pints
   ③ 9–12 pints

3. **What was the original purpose of the Leaning Tower of Pisa?**

   ① Prison
   ② Bell tower
   ③ Military lookout

4. **On what show did Charlie Sheen star as Charlie Harper?**

   ① *Two and a Half Men*
   ② *George Lopez*
   ③ *Cold Case*

5. **Neil Young was born in which country?**

   ① England
   ② Canada
   ③ United States

6. **Who introduced the poetic form of a dramatic monologue to literature?**
    ① Alfred, Lord Tennyson
    ② T. S. Eliot
    ③ Robert Browning

7. **Ackee (a fruit) and saltfish is the national dish of which country?**
    ① Jamaica
    ② Sweden
    ③ Czechoslovakia

8. **In billiards, what color is the 5 ball?**
    ① Blue
    ② Orange
    ③ Red

9. **What was the first virus ever discovered (1879)?**
    ① Tobacco mosaic virus
    ② Rabies virus
    ③ Bubonic plague

10. **In *Aliens*, which character used the shotgun for close encounters?**
    ① Pvt. Drake
    ② Ripley
    ③ Cpl. Hicks

QUIZ 56

1. **What 2013 film stars Jennifer Garner and Matthew McConaughey?**
    - ① *The Fifth Estate*
    - ② *Her*
    - ③ *Dallas Buyers Club*

2. **P-Nut is a member of which band?**
    - ① Oasis
    - ② 311
    - ③ Indigo Girls

3. **Who, upon seeing a young Pablo Picasso's talent, declared he himself would not paint again?**
    - ① Pablo's father
    - ② John Lennon
    - ③ Leonardo da Vinci

4. **Whose claim to the Falkland Islands does the United States not recognize?**
    - ① Australia
    - ② Argentina
    - ③ Japan

5. **What makes up about 70 percent of most living things?**
    - ① Carbon
    - ② Nitrogen
    - ③ Water

6. **In badminton, what refers to the feathered section of a shuttlecock?**
   ① Skirt
   ② Petticoat
   ③ Dress

7. **Earl Grey tea is blended with oil extracted from what fruit?**
   ① Bergamot orange
   ② Lemon
   ③ Papaya

8. **How many total wedges or spaces are there on the wheel in *Wheel of Fortune*?**
   ① 32
   ② 24
   ③ 20

9. **What is Moby's real name?**
   ① Richard James Hall
   ② Richard D. James
   ③ Richard Melville Hall

10. **Which major department store chain filed for bankruptcy in 1992?**
    ① Macy's
    ② JCPenney
    ③ Target

QUIZ 57 (TELEVISION 2)

1. **What is the principal's name played by Iqbal Theba in *Glee*?**

   ① Principal Slope
   ② Principal Figgins
   ③ Principal Wormer

2. **Which actor plays Doug Stamper, Frank Underwood's loyal chief of staff, in the TV show *House of Cards*?**

   ① Michael Kelly
   ② Kevin Spacey
   ③ Corey Stoll

3. **Who plays Sookie Stackhouse on the series *True Blood*?**

   ① Dakota Fanning
   ② Anna Paquin
   ③ Selena Gomez

4. **Who hangs out at The Drunken Clam?**

   ① Homer Simpson
   ② Drew Carey
   ③ Peter Griffin

5. **What was the term used at the end of every *G. I. Joe* show?**

   ① And knowing is half the battle
   ② Right is might
   ③ Until next time

6. **What year did the TV show**
   Max Headroom premier?

   ① 1965
   ② 1987
   ③ 1991

7. **Which celebrity sued for copyright**
   infringement on _Family Guy_, but lost
   her lawsuit?

   ① Carol Burnett
   ② Zsa Zsa Gabor
   ③ Roseanne Barr

8. **On _Survivor: Fiji_ what did Yau-Man Chan**
   give Dreamz Herd in exchange for his vote?

   ① A bag of rice
   ② Half his winnings
   ③ A car

9. **What are the first names of the lead**
   characters in _Rizzoli & Isles_?

   ① Angela and Chrissy
   ② Kate and Tina
   ③ Jane and Maura

10. **Which _Torchwood_ actor has played The**
    Marshal, a bounty hunter, in the series _The_
    Man in the High Castle?

    ① Peter Capaldi
    ② Burn Gorman
    ③ Simon Poland

QUIZ 58

1. **On what show did Jon Lovitz use the phrase "Yeah, that's the ticket"?**
   - ① *Seinfeld*
   - ② *Saturday Night Live*
   - ③ *Cheers*

2. **Which Adele single from 2011 begins "There's a fire starting in my heart"?**
   - ① "Rumor Has It"
   - ② "Rolling in the Deep"
   - ③ "Love Song"

3. **In 1973, what caused long lines at the gas pumps in the USA?**
   - ① Arab oil embargo
   - ② Cheap gas prices
   - ③ Trucker strike

4. **The beluga whale is what color as an adult?**
   - ① Silver
   - ② White
   - ③ Black

5. **How high is the badminton net in the center?**
   - ① 7 feet
   - ② 3 feet
   - ③ 5 feet

6. **What is the goal for teens in the President's Challenge Active Lifestyle program?**
   - ① Lose 20 pounds
   - ② Run a 6-minute mile every day
   - ③ Active 60 minutes a day, 5 days a week

7. **What ingredients when added to hollandaise sauce make sauce Béarnaise?**
   - ① Fish fumet and basil
   - ② Wine and tarragon
   - ③ Lemon thyme and port wine

8. **How was René Magritte's first solo art show received by the people of Brussels?**
   - ① With anger
   - ② Greatly
   - ③ Badly

9. **The 2006 movie *Rescue Dawn* is the true story of a U.S. pilot shot down over what country?**
   - ① North Korea
   - ② Laos
   - ③ Soviet Union

10. **Which Croatian tennis player claimed his maiden Grand Slam title at the 2014 US Open?**
    - ① Ivo Karlovic
    - ② Borna Coric
    - ③ Marin Cilic

QUIZ 59

1. **The musician Twiggy Ramirez is from which group?**
   ① Green Day
   ② Marilyn Manson
   ③ Metallica

2. **Topher Grace appeared on which TV show as Eric Forman?**
   ① *8 Simple Rules*
   ② *I'm with Her*
   ③ *That '70s Show*

3. **With which fellow painter did Salvador Dali become friends while in Paris?**
   ① Pablo Picasso
   ② Andy Warhol
   ③ Henri Matisse

4. **What strangely named type of mackerel is also known as an Ono in Hawaii?**
   ① Wahoo
   ② Woowoo
   ③ Wackawacka

5. **In hurling, what is the name of the wooden stick used to hit the ball?**
   ① Sliotar
   ② Hurley
   ③ Bas

6. **The sun's mass is approximately how many times as great as Earth's?**

   ① 330,000
   ② 10,000
   ③ 1,000,000

7. **How old was Dr. Seuss when he wrote about the Grinch?**

   ① 51
   ② 54
   ③ 53

8. **What does the "circle of Willis" relate to?**

   ① Aqueous flow in the eye
   ② Behavioral disorder
   ③ Blood supply to the brain

9. **When did the stock market crash called "Black Friday," which was fueled by gold speculation, occur?**

   ① September 24, 1869
   ② October 1987
   ③ November 1929

10. **Who was the first Naïve painter to achieve recognition in the USA?**

    ① John Kane
    ② Grandma Moses
    ③ Horace Pippin

QUIZ 60

1. **Which of these actors is the oldest?**
   1. Brad Pitt
   2. Tom Cruise
   3. Keanu Reeves

2. **What is the name of the girl who played Michael's girlfriend in the music video *Thriller*?**
   1. Naomi Campbell
   2. Jennifer Lopez
   3. Ola Ray

3. **Mexican artist Diego Rivera painted huge murals on the walls of what structures?**
   1. Public buildings
   2. Churches
   3. Prison cells

4. **In A. A. Milne's book *Winnie the Pooh*, what name is on the outside of Winnie the Pooh's house?**
   1. Pooh
   2. Sanders
   3. Bear

5. **A phytotoxin is a poison produced from what?**
   1. Plants
   2. Industrial waste
   3. Tree frogs

6. **Who performed "America the Beautiful" at game 5 of the 2015 World Series?**

   ① Snoop Dogg
   ② Tony Bennett
   ③ Jimmy Buffett

7. **What number uniform did LeBron James wear for the 2014–15 Cavs?**

   ① 23
   ② 00
   ③ 2

8. **A 1634 Spanish decree called what city "Key to the New World and Rampart of the West Indies"?**

   ① San Juan
   ② Port of Spain
   ③ Havana

9. **Pablo Picasso's *Guernica* was painted using only what 3 colors?**

   ① Orange, purple, and brown
   ② Pink, yellow, and red
   ③ Black, white, and gray

10. **Which director portrayed Jordan Belfort's father, Max, in the 2013 film *The Wolf of Wall Street*?**

    ① Rob Reiner
    ② Spike Jonze
    ③ Jon Fabreau

QUIZ 61

1. **What film had the most nominations at the 75th Golden Globe Awards in 2018?**
   ① *The Disaster Artist*
   ② *The Shape of Water*
   ③ *Lady Bird*

2. **Which famous poet who wrote "On the Pulse of Morning" died in 2014?**
   ① Maya Angelou
   ② Robert Frost
   ③ Charles Bukowski

3. **How tall was the single piece of marble Michelangelo used to create *David*?**
   ① 12 feet
   ② 17 feet
   ③ 3 feet

4. **Where did James Cook explore in the 1700s?**
   ① South Pacific
   ② Antarctica
   ③ Siberia

5. **Who was the manager of the 2016 Minnesota Twins?**
   ① Don Mattingly
   ② Paul Molitor
   ③ Craig Counsell

6. **Which of the following was *not* a component of the original Dow Jones Industrial Average?**

   ① American Sugar
   ② American Tobacco
   ③ Standard Oil

7. **What was the original name of Diet Pepsi?**

   ① Patio Diet Cola
   ② TaB
   ③ Pepsi Light

8. **Which Apollo flight was the first to orbit the moon?**

   ① *Apollo 13*
   ② *Apollo 8*
   ③ *Apollo 1*

9. **The term "red herring" comes from which sport?**

   ① Hunting
   ② Sailing
   ③ Track and field

10. **What was Wilma Flintstone's maiden name?**

   ① Pebblemire
   ② Rockingham
   ③ Slaghoople

QUIZ 62

1. **What show asks "Is that your final answer?"**
    ① *Deal or No Deal*
    ② *Jeopardy!*
    ③ *Who Wants to Be a Millionaire?*

2. **Who starred in the 1991 remake of *Cape Fear*?**
    ① Robert De Niro
    ② Nick Nolte
    ③ Tom Hanks

3. **Which band did Mick Taylor leave to join The Rolling Stones?**
    ① Fleetwood Mac
    ② John Mayall's Bluesbreakers
    ③ Cream

4. **What was another name for a female World War I spy also known as "Agent H-21"?**
    ① Mata Hari
    ② Rose Greenhow
    ③ Tokyo Rose

5. **Mariano Rivera approaches the mound to the tune of which Metallica song?**
    ① "Enter Sandman"
    ② "Ride the Lightning"
    ③ "Fuel"

6. **A 1920 Frida Kahlo painting shows people sitting outside waiting for what?**

① The rain
② The bus
③ An answer

7. **What is the hobby of collecting of old security and stock certificates called?**

① Philately
② Stockophily
③ Scripophily

8. **What color are the caps of regular Snapple teas?**

① Blue
② Silver
③ Green

9. **What is any two-handed handplant in snowboarding called?**

① Handy
② Bonking
③ Ho Ho

10. **Which element was the first ever artificially created?**

① Berkelium
② Technetium
③ Curium

QUIZ 63

1. **Leonardo da Vinci's *Vitruvian Man* depicts a man drawn within which shapes?**
   ① Triangle and hexagon
   ② Rectangle and star
   ③ Circle and square

2. **Which "Friend" asks the question "How you doin'?"**
   ① Joey
   ② Chandler
   ③ Ross

3. **Who sings this lyric: "Oh, but I need some time off, from that emotion"?**
   ① "Some Like It Hot" by Power Station
   ② "The Crying Game" by Boy George
   ③ "Faith" by George Michael

4. **Which film featured Daniel Day-Lewis and Emma Thompson?**
   ① *In the Name of the Father*
   ② *A River Runs Through It*
   ③ *Affliction*

5. **What organic material is formed from decaying organisms that mix with rocks?**
   ① Dirty material
   ② Humus
   ③ Sand

6. **What did the Gutta golf ball replace?**
   ① The rubber ball
   ② The Featherie
   ③ The wooden ball

7. **Which Caribbean island in the Lesser Antilles is shared by 2 countries?**
   ① Curaçao
   ② St. Barts
   ③ Saint-Martin

8. **In which state can you find Wendy's headquarters?**
   ① Ohio
   ② Texas
   ③ Kentucky

9. **What was the focus of the Geometric period of ancient Greek art?**
   ① Colors
   ② Shapes
   ③ Textures

10. **Where in the USA is *Better Call Saul* set?**
    ① Phoenix
    ② San Jose
    ③ Albuquerque

QUIZ 64

1. **In 2005, who won the MTV Best New Artist Award for "Mr. Brightside"?**

   ① The Killers
   ② Nirvana
   ③ Weezer

2. **What powerful, cube-shaped energy source was stolen by Loki in the 2012 superhero film *The Avengers*?**

   ① Aether
   ② Tesseract
   ③ Orb

3. **Who entered rehab in 2011 following his split from Courteney Cox?**

   ① Matthew Perry
   ② Luke Perry
   ③ David Arquette

4. **What size shoe does Shaquille O'Neal wear?**

   ① Size 22
   ② Size 18
   ③ Size 32

5. **Which of the following is an order of reptile?**

   ① Amphibian
   ② Swimming
   ③ Crocodilia

6. **What famous woman was a radio actress before gaining political power?**

   ① Eva Perón
   ② Jackie Kennedy
   ③ Susan B. Anthony

7. **When were the terms "weblog" and "weblogger" added to the Oxford English Dictionary?**

   ① June 2000
   ② March 2003
   ③ September 2005

8. **Which American president sang "Will the Circle Be Unbroken" at the Grand Ole Opry?**

   ① Jimmy Carter
   ② Richard Nixon
   ③ Ronald Reagan

9. **What is the Count of Monte Cristo's real name?**

   ① Dantes
   ② Villefort
   ③ Faria

10. **How did Ronda Rousey win at the February 22, 2014, UFC 170 event?**

    ① Decision
    ② KO
    ③ TKO

QUIZ 65

1. **Which art style emphasizes the precise rendering of subject matter in a realistic manner?**

   ① Expressionism
   ② Photorealism
   ③ Impressionism

2. **People in the audience of which show love to hear "Come on down"?**

   ① *Deal or No Deal*
   ② *Jeopardy!*
   ③ *The Price Is Right*

3. **What does the number 3 that Dwyane Wade wears on his jersey represent?**

   ① Holy Trinity
   ② His birthday
   ③ Family size

4. **What scripture does Jules quote before he kills someone in *Pulp Fiction*?**

   ① John 23
   ② Ezekiel 25
   ③ Matthew 25

5. ***Ms. Kelly* was the sophomore CD release by a member of what girl group?**

   ① Destiny's Child
   ② The Pussycat Dolls
   ③ The Spice Girls

6. **When was the first Hollister clothing store opened?**
   ① 2000
   ② 1992
   ③ 1985

7. **Which Rice Krispies character appeared on the box before any others?**
   ① Crackle
   ② Pop
   ③ Snap

8. **Which Bavarian castle did Walt Disney model Cinderella's after?**
   ① Mad King Ludwig's
   ② Glockenspiel
   ③ Neuschwanstein

9. **Who won the American League Cy Young Award in 1999?**
   ① Pedro Martinez
   ② Tom Glavine
   ③ Pat Hentgen

10. **The homely bar wench in *Shrek 2* is voiced by whom?**
    ① Roseanne Barr
    ② Bea Arthur
    ③ Larry King

QUIZ 66

1. **This fashion label/retailer takes its name from a small nation dependent on one crop.**
   ① Abercrombie & Fitch
   ② Banana Republic
   ③ Mavi Jeans

2. **Which of these spins the fastest?**
   ① LP
   ② 45
   ③ 78

3. **Which of the following legendary astronauts did *not* walk on the moon?**
   ① Neil Armstrong
   ② Buzz Aldrin
   ③ Gus Grissom

4. **Fresco is a technique involved in which type of painting?**
   ① Oil
   ② Mural
   ③ Portrait

5. **Maze War, Spasim, and Doom are examples of what type of gaming?**
   ① Action adventure
   ② First-person shooter
   ③ Open world

6. **In Jim Garrison's trial against Clay Shaw in 1968, this famous film was shown for the first time to the public?**

   ① The Zapruder film
   ② The moon landing
   ③ The Rolling Stones at Altamont

7. **A stuffed quahog is constructed around which mollusk?**

   ① Mussel
   ② Oyster
   ③ Clam

8. **In *Catcher in the Rye*, Holden Caulfield wonders where these winged creatures in Central Park go in the winter.**

   ① Pigeons
   ② Birds
   ③ Ducks

9. **Johnny Cash recorded 2 albums at U.S. prisons. Which of these institutions did he *not* perform at?**

   ④ San Quentin Prison
   ⑤ Folsom Prison
   ⑥ Alcatraz Prison

10. **Which of the following is *not* a form of a leafy cabbage?**

    ① Kale
    ② Arugula
    ③ Bok choy

QUIZ 67

1. **The first officially recorded baseball game was played on June 19, 1846, in this town.**

   ① Hoboken, New Jersey
   ② Cooperstown, New York
   ③ Hartford, Connecticut

2. **The WPA was created as part of FDR's New Deal and employed some of America's most famous photographers. Which of the below was *not* associated with the program?**

   ① Dorothea Lange
   ② Ansel Adams
   ③ Walker Evans

3. **The first commercially produced compact discs appeared for sale on October 1, 1982, in which country?**

   ① Japan
   ② United States of America
   ③ United Kingdom

4. **Bob Dylan, Ozzy Osbourne, and Cheap Trick have all released live albums recorded at this legendary venue.**

   ① Madison Square Garden
   ② Budokan
   ③ The Fillmore East

5. **This Woody Allen film is an homage to one his primary influences, Ingmar Bergman.**

   ① *Manhattan*
   ② *Interiors*
   ③ *Crimes and Misdemeanors*

6. **A group of these birds is appropriately referred to as a "pandemonium."**
   ① Sparrows
   ② Owls
   ③ Parrots

7. **The process of applying gold or gold specks to an illuminated manuscript is known as:**
   ① Burnishing
   ② Illumination
   ③ Coloring

8. **Georgios Kyriacos Panayiotou is the given name of which of these famous singers?**
   ① George Harrison
   ② Boy George
   ③ George Michael

9. **Which is the only state name that can be typed on a single line of keys on the QWERTY keyboard?**
   ① Utah
   ② Ohio
   ③ Alaska

10. **Which of the following is the name of the dot above a lowercase i or j?**
    ① Iota
    ② Tittle
    ③ Bot

QUIZ 68 (MOVIES)

1. **What movie is about a studio executive being blackmailed by a writer?**
   ① *Fried Green Tomatoes*
   ② *The Player*
   ③ *Fear and Loathing in Las Vegas*

2. **Which director, known for *Bad Boys* and *The Rock*, worked on 2007's *Transformers*?**
   ① Michael Bay
   ② J.J. Abrams
   ③ Peter Jackson

3. **In the 1999 movie *The Matrix*, what actor played the part of Morpheus?**
   ① Samuel L. Jackson
   ② Laurence Fishburne
   ③ Denzel Washington

4. **In what film did Spike Lee play Mookie?**
   ① *Ronin*
   ② *Jungle Fever*
   ③ *Do the Right Thing*

5. **Who portrayed Sid Vicious in the acclaimed film *Sid and Nancy*?**
   ① Gary Oldman
   ② Tim Roth
   ③ Richard E. Grant

6. **Which of these feature films was *not* a Pixar production?**

   ① *Shark Tale*
   ② *Finding Nemo*
   ③ *The Incredibles*

7. **In *Contact*, what causes the first machine to be destroyed?**

   ① Electrical failure
   ② Meteor shower
   ③ A suicide bomber

8. **In *Pulp Fiction*, how long was Vincent's car out of storage when it was keyed?**

   ① 5 days
   ② 2 hours
   ③ 3 days

9. **In *Field of Dreams*, at what baseball stadium did Terrance Mann say he always wanted to play?**

   ① Fenway Park
   ② Ebbets Field
   ③ Yankee Stadium

10. **The 2014 sci-fi film *Interstellar* was inspired by the work of what theoretical physicist?**

    ① Stephen Hawking
    ② Kip Thorne
    ③ Carl Sagan

QUIZ 69 (ROCK MUSIC)

1. **What was the middle name of Nirvana's Kurt Cobain?**
   - ① Dale
   - ② Daniel
   - ③ Donald

2. **What kind of car is the name of a 2012 album by The Black Keys?**
   - ① El Camino
   - ② Trans-Am
   - ③ Corvette

3. **Who did U2's Bono say was "Picasso to me"?**
   - ① Bruce Springsteen
   - ② Bob Dylan
   - ③ Lou Reed

4. **Which Pink Floyd song is this lyric from: "Is there anybody in there, just nod if you can hear me"?**
   - ① "Money"
   - ② "Hey You"
   - ③ "Comfortably Numb"

5. **In Warren Zevon's classic song "Werewolves of London," who was "mutilated late last night"?**
   - ① Little old lady
   - ② Teacher
   - ③ Cop

6. **Who were the cowriters of the Eagles' hit "Take It Easy"?**

   ① Joe Walsh and Don Henley
   ② Phil Collins and Randy Meisner
   ③ Jackson Browne and Glenn Frey

7. **What was the name of The Yeah Yeah Yeahs' July 2007 EP release?**

   ① *Is Is*
   ② *Was Was*
   ③ *Is Not*

8. **What 2013 single by the Arctic Monkeys begins "Have you got color in your cheeks?"**

   ① "R U Mine?"
   ② "Do I Wanna Know"
   ③ "One for the Road"

9. **Whose album is titled *Good News for People Who Love Bad News*?**

   ① Evanescence
   ② Taking Back Sunday
   ③ Modest Mouse

10. **Which indie rock band reunited in 2013 to play a tour using songs from their *Aeroplane Over the Sea* album?**

   ① Neutral Milk Hotel
   ② The Minders
   ③ The Apples in Stereo

QUIZ 70 (ART)

1. **What are the cut-and-pasted images of Harlem Renaissance artist Romare Bearden called?**
   - ① Paintings
   - ② Monoliths
   - ③ Collages

2. **Which Italian artistic movement focused on showing life in the age of machines?**
   - ① Pop Art
   - ② Futurism
   - ③ Impressionism

3. **What type of subject matter is Mexican painter Frida Kahlo best known for?**
   - ① Self portraits
   - ② Still life paintings
   - ③ Landscapes

4. **Which artist came to the U.S. in 1944 and painted *Broadway Boogie-Woogie* shortly before his death?**
   - ① Marcel Duchamp
   - ② Piet Mondrian
   - ③ Pablo Picasso

5. **What was the last painting Vincent van Gogh painted before he killed himself?**
   - ① *At the Moulin Rouge*
   - ② *Starry Night*
   - ③ *Wheatfield with Crows*

6. **What is the condition of a surface displaying a lustrous, rainbow-like brightness called?**
   ① Shine
   ② Iridescence
   ③ Glow

7. **Pablo Picasso said that the best work was made for what moment in time?**
   ① The future
   ② The past
   ③ The present

8. **Which artist finally gave up painting in 1912 because of failing eyesight?**
   ① Cézanne
   ② Degas
   ③ Renoir

9. **In the late 1700s Francisco Goya took a job drawing for what type of royal factory?**
   ① Glassblowing
   ② Printing
   ③ Tapestry

10. **Which artist first adopted the word "assemblages" for works he made in 1953–54?**
   ① Dubuffet
   ② Picasso
   ③ Pollock

QUIZ 71

1. **What industry did John D. Rockefeller achieve his monopoly in?**
    ① Railroad
    ② Steel
    ③ Oil

2. **This is the only number whose letters are in alphabetical order when spelled out.**
    ① 1
    ② 8
    ③ 40

3. **Which of these cities is farthest west?**
    ① Los Angeles, California
    ② Reno, Nevada
    ③ Fresno, California

4. **The S. in Harry S. Truman stands for what?**
    ① Solomon
    ② Sandy
    ③ Nothing

5. **This phrase was added to The Pledge of Allegiance during the red scare in 1954 is?**
    ① Of the United States of America
    ② Under God
    ③ One nation

6. **Which band's name was taken from a candy bar?**
   ① Milhouse
   ② Red Hot Chili Peppers
   ③ Squirrel Nut Zippers

7. **Which of the following did *not* serve in the military?**
   ① John Wayne
   ② Johnny Cash
   ③ James Stewart

8. **This enormous underwater creature has 3 hearts.**
   ① Blue whale
   ② Octopus
   ③ Lion's mane jellyfish

9. **The first presidential memoir ever published was written by which president?**
   ① Richard Nixon
   ② Theodore Roosevelt
   ③ James Buchanan

10. **Pablo Picasso painted a famous picture depicting which bombed city?**
   ① London
   ② Brandenburg
   ③ Guernica

H-QUIZZING TIP

Always have fun!

QUIZ 72

1. **A group of these reptiles is appropriately referred to as a "quiver."**
    ① Cobras
    ② Vipers
    ③ Turtles

2. **Who is the old woman to whom Atticus makes Jem read in *To Kill a Mockingbird*?**
    ① Miss Stephanie
    ② Mrs. Radley
    ③ Mrs. Dubose

3. **The croissant, commonly thought of as a French pastry, was actually created in which country?**
    ① Austria
    ② Switzerland
    ③ Italy

4. **Who holds the record for fastest fastball ever pitched, at 105.1 miles per hour?**
    ① Nolan Ryan
    ② Aroldis Chapman
    ③ Roger Clemens

5. **What is the scale used to measure tornadoes?**
    ① The Foley Scale
    ② The Fahrenheit Scale
    ③ The Fujita Scale

6. **What must a meteor do in order to become a meteorite?**

   ① Travel through space at 300,000 mps
   ② Burn up in the Earth's atmosphere
   ③ Hit the Earth's surface

7. **How old was Marlon Brando at the time of his death in 2004?**

   ① 61
   ② 56
   ③ 80

8. **Ludwig van Beethoven suffered from which disease that eventually caused his deafness?**

   ① Addison's disease
   ② Tuberculosis
   ③ Plumbism (lead poisoning)

9. **Which male golfer has won the most championships?**

   ① Tiger Woods
   ② Ben Hogan
   ③ Jack Nicklaus

10. **On which Bob Dylan album did he perform a duet with Johnny Cash?**

    ① *Highway 61 Revisited*
    ② *The Freewheelin' Bob Dylan*
    ③ *Nashville Skyline*

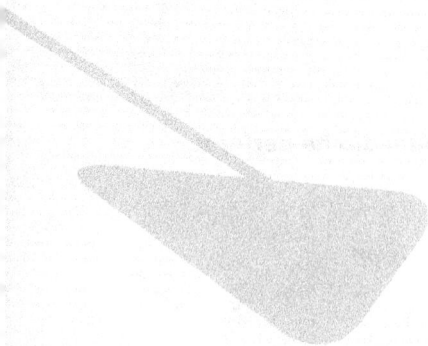

ANSWERS

QUIZ 1 ANSWERS

1. Hannah was **protesting on the White House property** against the proposed Keystone oil pipeline from Canada to the U.S. Gulf Coast.

2. The **backstroke** swimming style is faster than the breaststroke but it's slower than the butterfly.

3. **Douglas Adams** came up with the idea for the title of *The Hitchhiker's Guide to the Galaxy* while he was laying drunk under the stars.

4. **Juan Ponce de León** was reportedly trying to find the "Fountain of Youth."

5. **Decorative**: The Art Deco movement, from 1925 until the 1940s, was seen as elegant glamorous, functional, and modern.

6. **Chris Matthews** has been a White House speechwriter and aide in both houses of the U.S. Congress.

7. **"You Don't Know My Name"** was based on a true story.

8. **Sting**: Fans were able to have their names added to the lengthy credits of *The Lord of the Rings* for only $39.95.

9. **Kenny Perry** won the 2011 SAS Championship by a single stroke over John Huston and Jeff Sluman.

10. **Stalin**'s official cause of death was cerebral hemorrhage.

_____Correct

QUIZ 2 ANSWERS

1. **"I'm smarter than the average bear**." Yogi Berra displayed difficulty with arithmetic when he said, "I usually take a two-hour nap from one to four."

2. **Chemical weathering** is caused by atmospheric chemicals or those that are biologically produced.

3. **Mariah Carey**: The Fresh Air Fund is a charity that helps inner-city children have fun in less urban environments.

4. Darth Vader wasn't impressed with **Admiral Motti**'s faith.

5. **Canada:** In Avril Lavigne's song "My World," she sings about growing up in Napanee, "a five-thousand population town."

6. **Color**: Cézanne said, "There is no model; there is only color."

7. **Sarsaparilla**: The world headquarters for Anheuser-Busch is in St. Louis, Missouri.

8. **Germany**: The word "ozean" is German for ocean.

9. **Cricket**: A "googly" is delivered out of the back of the hand with the wrist 180 degrees to the ground and turned toward the batsman rather than away from the bat.

10. **Headache**: Migraine headaches are neurological conditions more common in women than in men.

_____Correct

QUIZ 3 ANSWERS

1. **The Smurfs**: Pop star Katy Perry was the voice of Smurfette in the film.

2. **Mycroft** solved such mysteries as "The Mazarin Stone" while his brother Sherlock Holmes was "missing."

3. **180 Degrees**: Since each eye does not have exactly the same view, depth perception in people covers 140 degrees of the field of vision.

4. **Tony Stewart** was the NEXTEL Cup Champion in 2005.

5. **Scotland**: Dolly the sheep died at the age of 6.

6. ***The Devil Wears Prada*** opened in theaters June 30, 2006.

7. **Canada** is the second largest land mass country in the world, just behind Russia.

8. **Kyudo**: Kobudo is the Okinawan art of weaponry and Nage Waza is a throw.

9. ***Man in White***, which is Cash's only novel, was about the Apostle Paul.

10. **Edna St. Vincent Millay**: The poem is "Childhood Is the Kingdom Where Nobody Dies."

_____Correct

QUIZ 4 ANSWERS

1. **Bow Wow Wow**: Lwin was born Myint Myint Aye to a Burmese father and an English mother in Rangoon.

2. **1976**: As a rough script from the second film shows, the actual name of the character in *Rocky* is Robert Balboa.

3. A Statue of **Giotto** is located at the Uffizi Gallery in Florence, Italy.

4. **Olive brine** can be used in place of or alongside vermouth.

5. **Athena** was said to have been born out of her father, Zeus's, head.

6. **2 months**: Charles Dickens' father makes an appearance as a fictional character in *Little Dorrit* and in *David Copperfield*.

7. **Cones**: The eye contains 6 to 7 million cones that provide color sensitivity.

8. The San Francisco Giants' last game at Candlestick Park ended in a 9-4 loss to the Los Angeles Dodgers on September 30, **1999**.

9. A "liquid market" is characterized by many bid and ask offers; a "**thin market**" has few offers.

10. Mayor Quimby pardoned one Robert **Underdunk** Terwilliger from prison.

_____Correct

QUIZ 5 ANSWERS

1. People with **O blood** type are universal donors while people with AB blood type are universal recipients.

2. **High pop fly**: The phrase is said to have originated in the 19th century and relates to an old-time grocer's method of getting canned goods down from a high shelf.

3. *In Living Color:* Dancer Carrie Ann Inaba has toured with pop superstars Madonna and Ricky Martin.

4. The 1996 comedy *The Birdcage* was a remake of the Franco-Italian film *La Cage aux Folles* and starred Robin Williams.

5. "**Lucy in the Sky with Diamonds**" was inspired by a drawing that John Lennon's son, Julian, drew in school.

6. **Holy water**: William Rowe invented a cigarette-vending machine in 1926.

7. **Onion**: According to an old English rhyme, the thickness of an onion skin can help predict the severity of a coming winter.

8. **The Featherie** golf ball was made of a wet leather casing stuffed with feathers, which shrunk to a hard, compact ball.

9. Demi Lovato appeared on *Barney & Friends* as Angela in seasons 7 and 8.

10. **Jeff Talley and Walter Smith**: The girl who portrayed the daughter of Bruce Willis in the movie *Hostage* was his real-life daughter Rumer.

_____Correct

QUIZ 6 ANSWERS

1. **37**: Will Smith was nominated for an Oscar for playing Ali in the 2001 film *Ali*.

2. **The Tennessee Titans** were formerly known as the Houston Oilers.

3. **Pack**: In roller derby, each jammer's goal is to get through or around the pack.

4. **Jimmy Walker** attended Baylor University in Waco, Texas.

5. **Jonathon Quick** posted a 16-4 record with a 1.41 GAA, a .946 save percentage, and 3 shutouts during the 2011–12 NHL playoffs.

6. **Badminton**: Jarkko Nieminen and Anu Weckstrom were married on June 11, 2005.

7. **Australia**

8. **Malaria**: Approximately 300 million people worldwide are affected by malaria and between 1 to 1.5 million people die from it every year.

9. **Arlington** beat out Indianapolis, Indiana, and Glendale, Arizona, to become host of the 2011 Super Bowl.

10. **1974**: As of 2006, Dallara is the manufacturer of the majority of Formula 3 cars seen on the track.

_____Correct

QUIZ 7 ANSWERS

1. **Goldie Hawn**: While growing up Kate Hudson's brother called her "Hammerhead."

2. *Physical Graffiti* was released in March 1975 and was certified gold within a week.

3. **The French Tricolour**: Eugene Delacroix's painting *Liberty Leading the People* commemorated the July Revolution of 1830.

4. **Pinot Noir**: The American winemaker Andre Tchelistcheff said, "God made cabernet sauvignon whereas the devil made pinot noir."

5. **Reykjavik** lies on Faxa Bay in southwestern Iceland.

6. **Johan Santana** won the Cy Young Award in 2004 and 2006.

7. **Atlanta**: Jennifer Hudson was born on September 12, 1981.

8. **Charlie and Dennis**: *It's Always Sunny in Philadelphia* was created and developed by Rob McElhenney, Glenn Howerton, and Charlie Day, who also star on the show.

9. **Francis Bacon**: Margaret Thatcher described Bacon as "that man who paints those dreadful pictures."

10. *The Wall Street Journal* is the popular English-language international daily newspaper published by Dow Jones & Company.

_____Correct

QUIZ 8 ANSWERS

1. **Running and cycling:** The order of triathlons is usually swim, cycle, and run although some professional sprint triathlons vary.

2. **Silent Bob** first appeared in the slacker comedy *Clerks* and is played by Kevin Smith.

3. **Monkey Man**: Though in the spirit of a Springsteen song, Monkey Man starred in the epic song "Tweeter and the Monkey Man" written by Bob Dylan for the Traveling Wilburys.

4. **6**: The Original Six era of the NHL began in 1942 and lasted 25 years.

5. **Horse racing**: The bestselling writer of horse racing mysteries was the Queen of England's favorite author.

6. Key witnessed the bombing campaign on **Fort McHenry** from a British ship about 8 miles away. The British were unable to destroy the fort and gave up.

7. **Quenya**: Dothraki is spoken in *Game of Thrones* and Na'vi is the language in James Cameron's *Avatar*.

8. Pepsi was invented in 1898 and Coca-Cola was invented in 1886, while **Dr Pepper** was invented in 1885.

9. **Wood**: The Janka rating determines the hardness of wood by measuring the force required to embed a steel ball halfway into a sample of the wood.

10. The Steadicam made its first appearance on film during **Rocky**'s unforgettable run up the steps of the Philadelphia Museum of Art.

_____Correct

QUIZ 9 ANSWERS

1. **San Francisco**: Jann Wenner and Ralph J. Gleason founded *Rolling Stone* in 1967.

2. **Polaris** is the brightest star in the constellation Ursa Minor.

3. ***1984***: These 3 slogans are on the outside wall of "The Ministry of Truth."

4. Streep was nominated for Best Supporting Actress in ***The Deer Hunter***. She was nominated again the following year for *Kramer vs. Kramer*, and she won.

5. The sideburns were the creation of the aptly named **Ambrose Burnside**.

6. Spanning 3,365 miles, **Route 20** is the longest road in the United States.

7. **Taylor Swift** co-wrote all 11 songs on her self-titled debut cd.

8. Bushnell is considered one of the founding fathers of the video game industry, having created **Atari**.

9. **2**: Mike Timlin and Curt Schilling were both part of World Series-winning teams prior to 2004.

10. **The Old Lady of Threadneedle Street**: The Bank of England was established in 1694 to act as the English government's banker.

_____Correct

QUIZ 10 ANSWERS

1. **Dino** is identified as a "snorkasaurus" throughout the course of the series.

2. **1976**: Apple protected the Apple design patents by taking legal action against companies that manufactured look-alikes.

3. *The Little Mermaid* sits in the harbor; the story was written by Hans Christian Andersen.

4. **Aurora Australis** is the southern counterpart to the Aurora Borealis.

5. Terry Collins managed the **2015 Mets**.

6. **George Carlin** appeared as the first host both of *Fridays* and *Saturday Night Live*.

7. **They didn't move**: Georgia O'Keeffe is chiefly known for paintings of flowers, rocks, shells, animal bones and landscapes.

8. **Sunglasses:** Before becoming an actor, Johnny Depp was a musician in several garage bands and once worked as a ballpoint pen salesman.

9. American tennis player Serena Williams joined the pro tour in **1995**.

10. **Uranium** is more plentiful than gold or silver.

_____Correct

QUIZ 11 ANSWERS

1. **Japan** is the only country where sumo wrestling is practiced professionally.

2. **Alan Shepard** was the first and only golfer on the moon.

3. **Cells**: About half the cells in the body are bacteria, 10 percent make up the solid tissues, and the remainder are blood and lymph cells.

4. **Gertrude Stein** lived with her brother Leo in Paris, France, from 1903 to 1914.

5. **Dutch:** Rembrandt's greatest creative triumphs are seen in his self-portraits and biblical scenes.

6. **Nike**: Graphic design student Carolyn Davidson designed the famous Nike swoosh, earning $35 for it.

7. "**All Me**," a bonus track from Drake's third album *Nothing Was the Same*, features fellow rappers 2 Chainz and Big Sean.

8. **The Green Goblin** first appeared in "Amazing Spider-Man #14" in 1964.

9. *Heaven Help Us:* Patrick Dempsey's middle name is Galen.

10. This group formed at **Yale** in 1901 for the purpose of drinking.

_____Correct

QUIZ 12 ANSWERS

1. *The Devil's Own* was a movie about an Irish hitman.

2. **September**: "Papa Was a Rolling Stone" won 3 Grammy awards in 1973.

3. **John James Audubon** was an American artist and naturalist of the 19th century.

4. **L.L. Bean** is based in Freeport, Maine.

5. **Winston Churchill** and Princess Diana were both members of the Spencer family.

6. **Leaves, flowers, and vines**: Art Nouveau peaked in popularity at the turn of the 20th century.

7. *Love Boat:* Andy Warhol was the son of Czech immigrants. His name was originally Warhola.

8. **Billie Holiday** moved to Harlem with her mother when she was 12.

9. *Something's Got to Give:* Marilyn Monroe died with most of the film unfinished. It was never completed.

10. A unit of 5 bonds is also referred to as a "**round lot**."

_____Correct

QUIZ 13 ANSWERS

1. **Cannoli**s are made with either ricotta or mascarpone in the U.S.

2. **Fishing**: In 1999 alone, Iceland's fishermen caught a total of 1.7 million tons of fish.

3. **Squire**: The young King Arthur serves as Sir Kay's squire in the traditional tale of the sword in the stone that appears in literary works including *Le Morte d'Arthur* and *The Once and Future King*.

4. Nick Cannon reportedly filed divorce papers from **Mariah Carey** on December 12, 2014.

5. **Uncle Moe's Family Feedbag**: Matt Groening named the Simpson family after members of his own family, except for his character, which he named "Bart."

6. **Weight**: Diamond is the second most stable form of carbon after graphite.

7. **The Orange River** flows through South Africa.

8. **9 to 0**: Fan unrest caused forfeits at the Washington Senators final game in 1971 and nearly at Shea Stadium in 1973.

9. **Lisa Kudrow** appeared in the *Cheers* episode "Two Girls for Every Boyd."

10. **Mustafar**: *Star Wars: Episode III – Revenge of the Sith* was the only film of the 6 not nominated for an Academy Award for Best Visual Effects.

_____Correct

QUIZ 14 ANSWERS

1. *Jerry Maguire:* Tom Cruise started acting after being sidelined from his high school's wrestling team due to a knee injury.

2. The 2013 war drama film **The Book Thief** is a film adaptation of Markus Zusak's 2005 novel of the same name.

3. **Kelsey Grammer** played Frasier in both *Cheers* and *Frasier*.

4. **Lemurs**: Jada Pinkett Smith was the voice of Gloria the Hippo in the movie *Madagascar*.

5. *X-Men:* Actor Hugh Jackman is also known for his singing ability and appeared in a TV version of *Oklahoma!* in 1999.

6. Out of its 10 nominations, *The Godfather* won **3** Oscars.

7. **James Cagney** portrayed Lon Chaney.

8. **4th Grade**: In addition to several movies, Jack Black has appeared on the television series *The X-Files*.

9. **Harold Pinter** got Academy Award nominations for his screenplays for both *Betrayal* and *The French Lieutenant's Woman*.

10. **King Vidor**: *The Fountainhead* was the only collaboration between Gary Cooper and King Vidor.

_____Correct

QUIZ 15 ANSWERS

1. **Domestic violence:** The actor had previously been charged with misdemeanor domestic violence after a fight in July 2009 with his wife.

2. **Vietnam War**: The 1976 film *Taxi Driver* takes place on the streets of New York City.

3. **Cartilage** is fibrous, elastic, and lightweight.

4. **Astor**: They also have a street in Manhattan named for them, Astor Place.

5. Mandela spent **27** years in prison before he was set free by South African President F.W. de Klerk in 1990.

6. *Glamour* magazine is published in 17 different languages for distribution around the world.

7. **Leonardo da Vinci by 23 years**; he lived to be 67 years old.

8. **Mathematics**: Christina Yang is played by Sandra Oh.

9. **Ignatius J. Reilly** is a character in John Kennedy Toole's *A Confederacy of Dunces*.

10. **Bart**: Tom Petty was one of the few traditionalist rock and rollers who embraced music videos.

_____Correct

QUIZ 16 ANSWERS

1. **Peter the Great** created the city of St. Petersburg, later Petrograd and Leningrad, to modernize and westernize the Russian state.

2. The uvula, a piece of tissue dangling in the **throat**, can be involved in snoring and is used for the guttural sound in some languages.

3. **Muhammad Ali** was also nicknamed "The Mouth" and "The Greatest."

4. On **_Arrested Development_**, George Michael works in the banana stand.

5. "It is Greek to me" was said by **Julius Caesar** in _The Tragedy of Julius Caesar_.

6. **Miley Cyrus**: "50 Ways to Leave Your Lover" was originally released in 1975.

7. **Olsen**.

8. **Steve Case** resigned from AOL-Time Warner's board of directors in 2006.

9. In Game 4 of the **1947** World Series Bill Bevens was one out away from throwing a no-hitter.

10. **Corner Area**: A corner kick leading to a header goal is called a "Dream Sequence" because of its dreamlike perfection.

_____Correct

QUIZ 17 ANSWERS

1. **9**: Martina Navratilova won the Wimbledon Mixed Doubles title in 2003 to give her a tie for the record of 20 Wimbledon titles.

2. **40 pounds**: The skin is the largest human organ, accounting for about 16 percent of body weight.

3. **United Nations** headquarters is located in New York City.

4. **Uma Thurman** divorced Gary Oldman in 1992.

5. **Major**: Christopher Walken mentions it at least twice while he is talking to young Butch about the watch.

6. **House of Parliament**: HP Sauce is a dark brown, fruity but savory sauce used in a similar way to mustard.

7. **Denmark**: Old Zealand is an island in Denmark.

8. **Hygrometer:** A hygrograph records water vapor in the atmosphere measured by a hygrometer.

9. **Patriots**: Bill Belichick formerly served as an assistant coach with the New York Giants.

10. **2**: Guitarist The Edge and bassist Adam Clayton were born in England.

_____Correct

QUIZ 18 ANSWERS

1. **The History Channel**: *The Sopranos* was created by David Chase.

2. **Tempering** results in chocolate that sets firm and shiny when it returns to room temperature.

3. **Egypt** captured, then nationalized, the Suez Canal.

4. **1996**: Although Derek Jeter received a scholarship to attend the University of Michigan, he chose to pursue a baseball career instead of college.

5. **River**: The Mississippi River is 3 feet deep at its headwaters and more than 200 feet deep in New Orleans.

6. Kandinsky then used the **colors and lines** on the canvas to convey his feelings about the music.

7. **1791**: The agreement was eventually signed under a large sycamore tree at 68 Wall Street.

8. **Ganet Bell**: A collection of poems published by the 3 sisters sold a mere 3 copies.

9. **Hallux**: "Morton's toe" is the condition in which the second toe is longer than the big toe.

10. **Traction control** enhances race car performance by preventing the wheels from spinning upon acceleration.

_____Correct

QUIZ 19 ANSWERS

1. **Carly Simon**'s father, Richard Simon, co-founded the Simon & Schuster publishing company.

2. **Salvador Dali** painted *The Persistence of Memory* in 1931.

3. **100**: The average human head has about 100,000 hair follicles that can each grow about 20 hairs over a person's lifetime.

4. **Pancho Villa** lived his early life as a fugitive before he fled to the U.S.

5. *Orca*: Robert Shaw played Quint in *Jaws*.

6. **Age 2**: Tiger Woods was seen on *The Mike Douglas Show* putting with Bob Hope.

7. **William Carlos Williams** was also a doctor.

8. *Fire Wheels*: Cream featured Eric Clapton and Ginger Baker.

9. Maria Sharapova's **loudest grunt** as of 2005 was 101.2 decibels.

10. In the third book of Stephen King's "The Dark Tower" series, Jake attended a private school named **Piper**.

_____Correct

QUIZ 20 ANSWERS

1. **Superman:** O'Neal also had the logo etched into the glass in his front door and in the grill of his Escalade.

2. **Salt**: Brine pools usually have a salinity greater than 5 percent.

3. Canada's only French-speaking province, **Quebec** voted to remain part of Canada in 1995.

4. **Spanish:** Matthew Morrison played Will Schuester on *Glee*.

5. When the *Mona Lisa* was X-rayed 3 **different drafts** were found under the finished painting.

6. **Mongols**.

7. **Climate Change**: The Concert for Diana in 2007 featured video tributes by former President Bill Clinton and Prime Minister Tony Blair.

8. **Seattle**.

9. A salto is a **gymnastics** flip or somersault in which the feet come up over the head and the body rotates around the waist's axis.

10. *Gunga Din* was written by Rudyard Kipling.

_____Correct

QUIZ 21 ANSWERS

1. **Harvard**: O'Brien wrote sketches for 3 years for *Saturday Night Live*.

2. A spaceship appeared over Johannesburg, **South Africa,** housing aliens nicknamed "The Prawns."

3. November 5 is known as "**Guy Fawkes** Day" in England, and is an occasion for bonfires, fireworks, and "penny for the guy" entreaties.

4. Magna Carta is the name of the charter agreed to by King John. The translation means **Great Charter** or The Great Charter of the Liberties of England.

5. **Stephen Edwin King** was born in Portland, Maine, in 1947.

6. **Catholic**: Caravaggio, Bernini, and Rembrandt were some of the many great artists of the Baroque period.

7. **Denny Crane**: During its 5 seasons, *Boston Legal* won 5 Emmy Awards, a Golden Globe Award, and a Peabody Award.

8. *Music of the Sun* was co-written by Rihanna.

9. **Ingolstadt**: Audi's corporate tagline is *Vorsprung durch Technik*, which translates into English as "Advantage Through Technology."

10. **Nabisco**: "Easy Cheese" is made in Wrightstown, Wisconsin.

_____Correct

QUIZ 22 ANSWERS

1. **Bruges, Belgium**: Tony Parker missed every one of his 3-point attempts in the 2005–06 NBA post-season playoffs against Dallas.

2. **7.4**: Markieff Morris is the twin brother of fellow 2011 NBA draftee Marcus Morris.

3. **LeBron James** played 4 seasons for the Miami Heat.

4. **Houston Rockets**: Dikembe Mutombo ended his NBA career in 2009 with 3,289 blocked shots, second only to Hakeem Olajuwon's 3,830.

5. Griffin recorded **63** double-doubles and 2 triple-doubles during his rookie season.

6. **Primoz Brezec** wore a size 17 basketball shoe.

7. **Kenneth Faried** is nicknamed "The Manimal" for his powerful playing style.

8. **Amare Stoudemire** was the ninth pick in the 2002 NBA Draft.

9. **Ralph Sampson**: David Robinson won 2 NBA titles with the San Antonio Spurs.

10. **Charlotte Bobcats**: Jan Vesely won 3 Serbian Cups with Partizan Belgrade between 2008 and 2011.

_____Correct

QUIZ 23 ANSWERS

1. **Lord Voldemort**'s name is partly inspired by the French word *mort*, which means death.

2. **Green Day** won the Record of the Year Grammy in 2006 for "Boulevard of Broken Dreams."

3. **Folk**: Terms that overlap with folk art are naïve art, pop art, outsider art, traditional art, self-taught art, and working-class art.

4. **GameBoy** sold over 100 million units during its first 20 years of availability.

5. **Mike Mussina**.

6. **7**: Hostess added squiggles to the icing on their cupcakes in 1950.

7. At age 15, Claude Monet made money selling **caricatures** at a local store for 10 to 20 francs apiece.

8. **Marcie**.

9. **A$AP Ferg**: "Low" was released on August 7, 2014, as the first single from Juicy J's fourth album *Pure THC: The Hustle Continues*.

10. **Swan**: Gloria Vanderbilt's signature was incorporated into the design of her jeans logo.

_____Correct

QUIZ 24 ANSWERS

1. **Matt Groening** served as editor of his college newspaper.

2. **Symmetry** involves similar, though not identical, elements that balance one another.

3. **The pillbox hat** took its simple lines from a pillbox, a small box used to store pills.

4. **South Africa** has only one time zone.

5. ***Dancing with the Stars***: Pittsburgh Steelers wide receiver Hines Ward is a 4-time Pro Bowler, 2-time Super Bowl Champion, and Super Bowl XL MVP.

6. In order to increase her value to Walt, Lydia suggests they ship to the **Czech Republic**, where there is a huge demand for meth.

7. ***La Bohème***: *Rent* pays tribute in the song "La Vie Bohème."

8. ***Nick of Time***: Johnny Depp was born in 1963.

9. **Esther Greenwood:** *The Bell Jar* is a stark narrative about depression.

10. **7**: A male giraffe may be 18 feet tall from hoof to crown.

_____Correct

QUIZ 25 ANSWERS

1. **Humans** are orca whales' only natural enemies.

2. **Blue**: The Cleveland Indians are nicknamed "The Tribe."

3. Lurch was the butler on *The Addams Family*.

4. Kevin Love's father is former NBA player Stan Love, brother of Mike Love of **The Beach Boys**.

5. **Acrophobia** is one of the 10 most common phobias.

6. **Van Halen** once held the record for highest paid rock group, earning one million for a brief gig at the US Festival.

7. **Flowers**: O'Keeffe hosted guests such as D.H. Lawrence, Ansel Adams, and Charles Lindbergh at her home, Ghost Ranch.

8. CNN started the **Quoted Everywhere** slogan in 2006.

9. **1967**: The score of the first Super Bowl was Green Bay 35, Kansas City 10.

10. **Bipolar Disorder**: The 2007 NIMH Genetics Initiative program included the first full scan of the entire human genetic code.

_____Correct

QUIZ 26 ANSWERS

1. **Cowboy Camp:** *Toy Story 2* was Tom Hanks' first sequel.

2. "Touch of Grey" was **the Grateful Dead**'s only Top 10 hit.

3. **Monochrome** images in neutral colors are known as grayscale or black and white.

4. *Lady Chatterly's Lover:* Lawrence was arrested in Germany in 1912 and accused of being a British spy.

5. **Oval**: The size of the Aussie Rules playing field is not fixed but is generally between 135–185m long and 110–155m wide.

6. **76 Years**: Halley's Comet was first seen in 240 BC.

7. Venus Williams won **Wimbledon** in 2000, then defended her title the next year.

8. **Broccoli** is high in vitamin C, vitamin A, calcium, fiber, and folic acid.

9. **Counting Machine**: IBM stands for International Business Machines.

10. **David Fincher** also directed the first 2 episodes of *House of Cards*.

_____Correct

QUIZ 27 ANSWERS

1. **Homer Simpson**: In 2006, "D'oh!" was listed as number 6 on *TV Land*'s list of the 100 greatest television catchphrases.

2. **Heat**: Infrared light is between the visible and microwave portions of the electromagnetic spectrum.

3. USA and the USSR worked on **détente** in the 1970s and 1980s.

4. **Wolfgang Puck** was a cook for Indiana National Bank in the mid-1970s.

5. **Antarctica** is both the coldest and driest continent on Earth.

6. *Silicon Valley* is partially inspired by Mike Judge's experiences as an engineer in the 1980s.

7. **Sam "Ace" Rothstein**: *Casino* used the promotional tagline of "No one stays at the top forever."

8. **Zoser**'s pyramid is not among the 3 at Giza but it is in Saqqara.

9. *Mister Roger's Neighborhood*: Michael Keaton worked with director Tim Burton on the 1988 movie *Beetlejuice* and appeared again in 1989's *Batman*.

10. Andy Warhol's earliest showings in New York at the Bodley Gallery were loose blotted ink drawings of **shoes**.

_____Correct

QUIZ 28 ANSWERS

1. *Hamlet* ends with the deaths of most of the main characters.

2. The name **Goya** was inspired by painter Francisco Goya whose paintings often featured guitars.

3. *The Young and the Restless*: David Hasselhoff is a huge singing star in Europe.

4. **Ogden Nash** used unconventional and punlike rhymes.

5. **"No soup for you!"**: Seinfeld originally aired from July 5, 1989, to May 14, 1998, on NBC.

6. **Saratoga chips**: The first potato chips were prepared by Native American chef George Crum in 1853.

7. **Margaret Thatcher:** Other female heads of state, including Golda Meir, have also been called "Iron Lady."

8. The **candy** desk was a tradition started in 1968 by California Sen. George Murphy.

9. **Birdland** was named after Charlie "Yardbird" Parker.

10. Proper bone health requires a good balance between cells that break down bone, **osteoclasts**, and cells that form bone, osteoblasts.

_____Correct

QUIZ 29 ANSWERS

1. The **front crawl** stroke is regarded as the fastest in competitive swimming.

2. **Mick Jagger**: "You're So Vain" topped *Billboard*'s Hot 100 chart for 3 weeks in 1973.

3. 100 percent of **Singapore** is on an island in the Straits of Malacca.

4. **Tail lights with LED rings**: "Altezza lights" are Euro-style tail assemblies that feature clear lenses, red driving and brake inserts, and chrome reflectors.

5. **Surrealism**: The *Surrealist Manifestos*, written by Andre Breton, defined the purpose of the group and included examples of surrealist works.

6. **21st**: *The Jetsons* first aired in 1962.

7. **16**: Joe Montana played college football at Notre Dame.

8. In cooking, to **coddle** food is to heat it in water kept just below the boiling point.

9. Pablo Picasso remained a loyal member of the **Communist Party** until his death.

10. **South Bend, Indiana**: The first class of College Football Hall of Fame inductees featured 54 people, including Jim Thorpe and Knute Rockne.

_____Correct

QUIZ 30 ANSWERS

1. **12**: The first season of *The Voice* took place at Warner Brothers Lot 16 in Los Angeles.

2. **The Warsaw Tavern**: *The Drew Carey Show* is set in Cleveland, Carey's hometown.

3. **The Maxx**: *Saved by the Bell* was broadcast on NBC from August 1990 until May 1993.

4. Larry believed that **Thor Olsen** slashed his tires.

5. **Buck** was a Shaggy Briard Sheepdog.

6. **Cowboy Bebop** is set in 2071 and follows a group of intergalactic bounty hunters.

7. At the age of 2, **Dominic Purcell** and his family moved from England to Sydney's Bondi.

8. **Richard Kiel**: Arnold Schwarzenegger was considered for the role of Hulk.

9. *12 oz. Mouse*: Adult Swim officially premiered on September 2, 2001, with the airing of the "Director's Cut" episode of Home Movies.

10. *Still Standing* first appeared in September 2002.

_____Correct

QUIZ 31 ANSWERS

1. **Iran**: Scholars still argue about the merits of using the name "Persia" to refer to either the entire country known to most of us as Iran, or at least to a province within it.

2. Fall Out Boy is the name of a fictional comic book sidekick on TV's **The Simpsons**.

3. **Billie Holiday**: *Lady Sings the Blues* got its title from the legendary singer's nickname, "Lady Day."

4. **San Marino** is known as the Postage Stamp country.

5. **Edward Hopper** painted his figures with a lack of unique features so that they would be anonymous and ordinary.

6. **George Lucas** was diagnosed with hypertension during the filming of the original 1977 *Star Wars*.

7. **Blade**: At least 85 percent of a table tennis racket blade by thickness shall be of natural wood.

8. **Africa**: *Mean Girls* was written by Tina Fey.

9. **Carlo Ventresca**, chamberlain to the late Pope, becomes Pope himself for 17 minutes.

10. *Batman Begins*: Katie Holmes and Tom Cruise made their marriage official in Los Angeles the day before their actual wedding ceremony in Italy.

_____Correct

QUIZ 32 ANSWERS

1. The 2013 biographical drama **Dallas Buyers Club** stars Matthew McConaughey, Jennifer Garner, and Jared Leto.

2. **Nelly Kim Furtado** was named after Soviet gymnast Nellie Kim.

3. Over his career, **Bernie Williams** has amassed 1,833 hits, 1,066 runs, 353 doubles, 226 home runs, and 998 RBIs, with a batting average of .308.

4. About 10 percent of Dalmatians are **deaf**; approximately 20 percent can only hear in one ear.

5. The phrase "so it goes" appears 116 times in **Slaughterhouse-Five**.

6. The famous **Tootsie Roll Pop** was born in 1931.

7. With over fifty adaptations of *A Christmas Carol* alone, **Charles Dickens** is the king of adaptations.

8. **Nick Kyrgios**: The 2014 Wimbledon Championships was the 138th edition of the tournament.

9. **1/9**: Icebergs that come to rest on the seabed in shallow water can become an ice island.

10. **William Wegman** is known for his photographs of his Weimaraners, which have become images of "pup culture."

_____Correct

QUIZ 33 ANSWERS

1. Morrison was arrested in **New Haven** for resisting arrest and disturbing the peace.

2. **Queens College**: Seinfeld's father was of Hungarian Jewish background and his mother was of Syrian Jewish background.

3. **1819**.

4. **Words**.

5. Aztecs believed that the **sun** sets every evening into the underworld and is born again every morning.

6. **Dungeons and Dragons**: Tim Duncan has tattoos of a jester and of Merlin the Magician.

7. Theodore Roosevelt created **Petrified Forest** National Monument on December 8, 1906.

8. **London**: The first official "gold fixing" occurred on September 12, 1919.

9. When buying "**gunpowder tea,**" it is important to look for shiny pellets because they indicate freshness.

10. Appearing both in *Batman Forever* and *Batman and Robin*, **Gossip Gerty** was played by Elizabeth Sanders.

_____Correct

QUIZ 34 ANSWERS

1. Bieber was arrested January 23 in **Miami** after an illegal street race with R&B singer Khalil Amir Sharieff.

2. **Dr. Amelia Brand:** Anne Hathaway almost suffered hypothermia while filming a water scene in Iceland for *Interstellar*.

3. Most **kiwi** fruit sold in the U.S. is grown in New Zealand.

4. **Liberia** was founded by former American slaves, and its capital, Monrovia, was named after President Monroe.

5. Ebbets Field, named after **Dodgers**' owner Charles Ebbets, was built on a former garbage dump at a cost of $750,000.

6. **Atlantic**: The Bermuda Islands are in the Sargasso Sea.

7. **Mary:** *South Park* was created by Trey Parker and Matt Stone.

8. **Aretha Franklin** is nicknamed "The Queen of Soul."

9. 2008 marked the 30th anniversary of the first publication of **Rumiko Takahashi**'s *Urusei Yutsara*.

10. Innovations was originally divided in the east and west **Communicores**.

_____Correct

QUIZ 35 ANSWERS

1. **Coco Chanel** was born Gabrielle Bonheur "Coco" Chanel in 1883.

2. **Romanticism** gained strength during the Industrial Revolution.

3. Nicklaus earned his nickname "**The Golden Bear**" because of his prominent mane of blond hair.

4. The mythological **Basilisk** was a lizardlike creature with the head of a rooster, and its gaze was supposedly deadly.

5. Most of the **grapes** sold in the U.S. come from Chile.

6. *Dumbo* opened in theaters in 1941.

7. **Pulp**: Joe Cocker was a friend of Jarvis Cocker but they are not related.

8. **Super Bowl 25**: Houston sang the anthem during the Bills-Giants clash in Super Bowl 25.

9. **Enterprise, Alabama,** built a monument to the boll weevil for making the farmers change their crops from cotton to peanuts.

10. **1983**: Windows was developed for IBM PC-compatible computers (based on Intel x86 architecture).

_____Correct

QUIZ 36 ANSWERS

1. **Carrie Bradshaw**: The real name of Mr. Big was not revealed until the series finale.

2. **The Black Crowes**: Kate Hudson's mother is the actress Goldie Hawn.

3. **Tzatziki**, served with Greek souvlaki, is made with cucumbers, garlic, and thick Greek yogurt.

4. **England**: John Callcott Horsley, a British narrative painter and a Royal Academician, designed the very first Christmas card in 1843.

5. In 1997 the Florida Marlins became the first wild card team to win the World Series, beating the **Cleveland Indians** in 7 games.

6. **Bull**: Camels have the reputation of being bad-tempered.

7. **Günter Grass'** major work is titled *The Tin Drum*.

8. **Baby Ruth** is a candy bar that is made of chocolate-covered peanuts and nougat.

9. Vera Wang designed an outfit for silver medalist **Nancy Kerrigan** for the 1994 Olympics.

10. In *Iron Man*, Tony Stark travels to **Afghanistan** to demonstrate a new weapons system.

_____Correct

QUIZ 37 ANSWERS

1. **Truth**: *Pravda* started publication in 1912.

2. **Caught the last train for the coast**: Don McLean's "American Pie" was dedicated to the memory of Buddy Holly.

3. **Burroughs** was trying to show off his marksmanship to friends but killed his wife with a single shot.

4. **Orion** is represented with his club and shield.

5. **Obama** is the 44th president of the United States.

6. **Charlie**: Director Stephen Chbosky also wrote the book and screenplay for the film.

7. **8**: And you call yourself a Simpson fan.

8. **Chuck Close**, known for large photorealistic portraits, retrained himself to paint with a brush strapped to his hand.

9. **Xavier Roberts**: The Cabbage Patch Kids were official mascots of the 1992 and 1996 U.S. Summer Olympic teams.

10. **Adamstown** is the capital of Pitcairn Island, the place where the *Bounty* mutineers eventually landed.

_____Correct

QUIZ 38 ANSWERS

1. **Japanese Pop Culture:** Harajuku is an area of Tokyo frequented by fashionable teenagers.

2. **Christina Aguilera** cowrote "Miss Independent," which was part of Kelly Clarkson's debut album.

3. **John Mayer** received the Hal David Starlight Award at the 37th Annual Songwriters Hall of Fame Induction Ceremony.

4. **Violin:** Dave Matthews released *Live at Red Rocks 8-15-95* in the fall of 1997.

5. **Michael Bublé** won 4 Juno Awards in 2006.

6. "Some Beach" was written by **Paul Overstreet** and Rory Lee Feek.

7. **Pink**: Adam Lambert came in second in the eighth season of *American Idol.*

8. **Aaliyah** signed with her uncle Barry Hankerson's Blackground Records label in 1993 at the age of 14.

9. **"Just the Way You Are"**: Bruno Mars provided guest vocals on two Top 10 hits in 2010: B.o.B's "Nothin' on You" and Travie McCoy's "Billionaire."

10. The video for **"Magic"** is centered around a magic show, based on a literal interpretation of the song.

_____Correct

QUIZ 39 ANSWERS

1. **Raekwon:** Wu-Tang Clan was voted the best rap group in the world by the magazine *The Source* in 2004.

2. **Snoop Dogg**: In 2007, Britney Spears released a new fragrance called Midnight Fantasy.

3. **Roman Zolanksi**: Minaj was the first female artist to be included on MTV's Annual Hottest MC List.

4. "**Can't Touch This**": Big Sean's first studio album, *Finally Famous*, sold 87,000 copies in its first week on sale in the United States.

5. **Adam "MCA" Yauch** died of cancer of the parotid salivary gland.

6. The video for "**Worst Behavior**" features cameo appearances by Turk, Juicy J, Project Pat, and Drake's father, Dennis Graham.

7. "**Nosetalgia**" features both artists rapping about the effects of cocaine on their childhoods.

8. "**I Mean It**" peaked at number 1 on the US *Billboard* Bubbling Under Hot 100 chart.

9. **Kendrick Lamar** also won Lyricist of the Year in both the 2012 and 2013 BET Hip Hop Awards.

10. **A$AP Ferg**'s album *Trap Lord* was supported by the singles "Work (Remix)," "Shabba," and "Hood Pope."

_____Correct

QUIZ 40 ANSWERS

1. **Lady Valarian** is a female Whiphid.

2. **Rodians** such as Greedo are reptilian humanoids with usually green skin, members of a traditionally violent culture.

3. **Chief Bast:** Grand Moff Tarkin was named after the Tarquins of ancient Rome.

4. **Race car driver:** George Lucas' first feature film was produced by Francis Ford Coppola.

5. The bounty hunter Bossk was a **Trandoshan**.

6. **Aa-23:** Carrie Fisher played Princess Leia in *Star Wars*.

7. *The Hidden Fortress:* Before *Star Wars*, George Lucas directed *American Graffiti*.

8. *Revenge of the Sith* was released in 2005.

9. **Mustafar:** *Revenge of the Sith* was the only film of the 6 not nominated for an Academy Award for Best Visual Effects.

10. **Togruta.**

_____Correct

QUIZ 41 ANSWERS

1. **Joey Archer** was born in 1938 and his career lasted from 1956 to 1967.

2. In addition to his 2 fights with Jonathan Barros, **Celestino Caballero** earned a decision win over Satoshi Hosano in 2011.

3. **Fernando Montiel** is trained by his father, former professional boxer Manuel Montiel.

4. **Sebastian Zbick**: As of July 2012, Felix Sturm had not been defeated since 2006.

5. After being knocked out by **Denis Lebedev** in 2011, Roy Jones Jr. lay unconscious on the canvas for several minutes.

6. **4th:** Victor Ortiz's 2011 fight with Floyd Mayweather ended in controversy, as the knockout punch came when Ortiz was looking away.

7. **Cuba:** The United States failed to win a single medal at the 2010 Summer Youth Olympics.

8. "**The Threat Is Real**": Sergio Martinez defeated Sergiy Dzinziruk by technical knockout in the 8th round of their 2011 fight.

9. **Yokohama:** Koki Kameda won a WBA Bantamweight title in 2010 by defeating Alexander Munoz.

10. Urbano Antillón was born in Nimiquipa, CH, **Mexico**.

_____Correct

QUIZ 42 ANSWERS

1. Martinez was a **catcher** who started his career with the Cleveland Indians in 2002.

2. **5 Games:** The Yankees defeated the Mets 4-1 in the 2000 "Subway Series."

3. **30 Home Runs:** Ken Griffey Jr. only hit 7 home runs after the All-Star Break in 1994, when he hit 33 before it.

4. **Francisco Liriano:** In his 16-year career, Joe Nathan accumulated 377 saves.

5. **10:** In 1995, Lou Piniella was named Manager of the Year.

6. **Lottery:** The Mets acquired Tom Seaver by winning a lottery that was held after the Atlanta Braves drafted him but broke signing regulations.

7. **Mickey Mantle** hit 3 home runs in the 1960 World Series.

8. **Gary Sheffield** won the Silver Slugger award four times.

9. **Cap Anson**, who had 3,418 career hits, was inducted into the Hall of Fame in 1939.

10. **Barry Bonds** won 5 Gold Gloves with the San Francisco Giants in the 1990s.

_____Correct

QUIZ 43 ANSWERS

1. The Cowboys' **Ring of Honor** includes "Dandy" Don Meredith.

2. **Terrell Davis** rushed for 2,008 yards and 21 touchdowns in 1998.

3. **Packers and Seahawks:** The Seahawks were given a touchdown on a play in the end zone that clearly looked like an interception.

4. **Oregon:** Dan Fouts was drafted by the San Diego Chargers in 1973 and played there for 15 seasons before retiring.

5. **Charles Haley** was born in 1964.

6. **Troy Aiken:** Tom Brady won the Super Bowl MVP in Super Bowls XXXVI and XXXVIII.

7. Former Raider **Marcus Allen** was traded to the Kansas City Chiefs to share the field with Joe Montana.

8. **2nd Round:** Boomer Esiason was the 38th player selected overall in the 1984 NFL Draft.

9. Tennessee Titans player **Eddie George** scored late in the third quarter against the Rams in Super Bowl XXXIV.

10. There are 32 women on the 2006 **Sea Gals** squad.

_____Correct

QUIZ 44 ANSWERS

1. Yani Tseng won **7** total LPGA events in 2011, including 2 majors.

2. **1932:** The USGA was founded in 1994.

3. **Olympic Club:** The United States did not host the U.S. Open in 2011 or 2010, when the tournament was played in Northern Ireland.

4. **Sergio Garcia**, who has been called "El Niño" since he was 14, would prefer his nickname to drop from use and to just be called "Sergio."

5. **Rory McIlroy** won his first major at age 22 at the U.S. Open.

6. Jim Furyk won the **Jack Nicklaus Trophy** for 2010 as the PGA Player of the Year.

7. In addition to the **AT&T Championship**, Fred Couples won the Constellation Energy Senior Players Championship in 2011.

8. **October:** In 2012 the PGA announced that future seasons would begin shortly after the Tour Championship of the previous year.

9. In 1972 **Pebble Beach** Golf Links hosted its first U.S. Open golf championship.

10. Golfer Tiger Woods won the **Ford Championship** March 6, 2005.

_____Correct

QUIZ 45 ANSWERS

1. **Evgeni Malkin** scored 109 points in only 75 games to lead all NHL scorers for the 2011–12 season.

2. The **Boston Bruins** defeated the Vancouver Canucks to win the Stanley Cup in 2011.

3. The **Pittsburgh Penguins** had 98 points for the 2014–15 season.

4. **Henrik Lundqvist** had a .930 save percentage for the 2011–12 season, tops among NHL starting goalies.

5. In 2009 some players and media members criticized **Alexander Ovechkin** for excessive goal celebrations.

6. **Saku Koivu** led with 8 assists and tied Finnish teammate Teemu Selanne for most points with 11.

7. **Ivan Vishnevskiy** began his professional hockey career with the Rouyn-Noranda Huskies.

8. **4**: The Los Angeles Kings never once faced elimination during the 2011–12 NHL playoffs.

9. **Sweden:** Winger Gabriel Landeskog was selected second overall in the 2011 NHL Entry Draft by the Colorado Avalanche.

10. **4**: NHL players David Booth, Frans Nielsen, Ryan Callahan, and David Steckel all scored penalty shot goals on October 30, 2010.

_____Correct

QUIZ 46 ANSWERS

1. **Australia:** *Mad Max* won 3 Australian Film Institute Awards in 1979, including Best Original Music Score.

2. **Maria Shriver** split from California governor Arnold Schwarzenegger after confirming that he had fathered a child with the family's longtime housekeeper.

3. **Led Zeppelin I:** Eva von Zeppelin threatened legal action against Led Zeppelin after seeing a photo of the *Hindenburg* on their first album.

4. **Well rounded:** Peter Paul Rubens was a 17th-century Flemish Baroque painter.

5. **Yeast extract:** The Marmite Food Company was set up in in 1902.

6. The **Henry James** novella was published in 1903 as part of a collection titled *The Better Sort*.

7. **Dactyl:** Astronomers announced the discovery of the first moon of an asteroid in 1994.

8. **10 kilometers:** A marathon swim is a nonstop open-water swim, requiring at least several hours of sustained effort to complete.

9. **Procter & Gamble:** Pringles are made from potatoes that have been cooked, mashed, dehydrated, and then reconstituted into a dough.

10. **Def Jam Recordings:** DJ Rev Run of Run-D.M.C. fame is the brother of Russell Simmons, who founded Phat Farm Clothing.

_____Correct

QUIZ 47 ANSWERS

1. In the Middle Ages, **rhetoric** was considered one of the 7 liberal arts.

2. Each color in a rainbow corresponds to a different **wavelength**.

3. NFL QBs Peyton and Eli **Manning** are the sons of former NFL QB Archie Manning.

4. **Alexander Dumas:** *The Count of Monte Cristo* was written in 1844.

5. **Fort-de-France:** The people of Martinique are French citizens with political and legal rights.

6. *La Gioconda:* The *Mona Lisa* was painted in 1519.

7. *Strictly Come Dancing* host Samantha Harris' parents created and produced one of the countries' first Renaissance festivals, King Richards Faire.

8. *Who's That Knocking at My Door?:* Martin Scorsese seriously considered entering the priesthood before he took up film.

9. In the video for the Foo Fighter's "**Learn to Fly**" a version of "Everlong" can be heard in the background.

10. **1903:** The winner of the first Tour de France bicycle race was Frenchman Maurice Garvin.

_____Correct

QUIZ 48 ANSWERS

1. **Hercules**' first appearance in the Marvel universe was in *Journey into Mystery Annual #1*.

2. Crosley Field was the **Reds**' park until its last game on June 24, 1970.

3. **Illegal Poker Ring:** Other A-list Hollywood celebs are also said to have played the no-limit Texas Hold'em games, including Leonardo DiCaprio, Ben Affleck, and Matt Damon.

4. **Thickly:** Rouen Cathedral is a Roman Catholic Gothic cathedral located in Rouen, in northwestern France.

5. The **Hawaiian** language consists of 10 vowels and 8 consonants and is spoken by fewer than 10,000 people.

6. "**Message in a Bottle**": The Tampa Bay Buccaneers and the Oakland Raiders played in the 2003 Super Bowl.

7. **Mumford & Sons** performed the song "I Will Wait" at the 2013 Grammy Awards.

8. **3:** The deserted island footage for *Cast Away* was shot on the mainland with a highway visible in the background; it was later digitally removed.

9. **Usemap="#Mapname":** Image maps allow graphics to be displayed on web pages with different parts of the image linking to different web pages.

10. **Mystery Fruitcake:** Betty Crocker is a made-up persona played by various actresses and illustrated variously in print.

_____Correct

QUIZ 49 ANSWERS

1. *Fast Times at Ridgemont High:* Nicolas Cage got his stage name from the comic book character Luke Cage.

2. **21**: Adele was first offered a recording contract after a friend posted her demo on MySpace in 2006.

3. **The Yellow Sea**'s name comes from the sand particles, originating from the Yellow River, that color its water.

4. **Stuart**: Mary Queen of Scots was executed for treason against Queen Elizabeth I.

5. In the movie, **Petey** the parakeet gets decapitated.

6. **Greece** has entered first since the beginning of the Olympics.

7. Acidic water dripping through **limestone** creates caves, caverns, and lost rivers.

8. **Francine Pascal** has been writing *Sweet Valley High* books since the 1980s.

9. **Mushroom**: Pieces of popped popcorn are called "flakes."

10. **Mike Kelley**: Pathetic art, or Abject art, came into vogue in the 1990s.

_____Correct

QUIZ 50 ANSWERS

1. **Earth art** works are frequently created in the open, away from civilization, and left to change and erode under natural conditions.

2. **Kate Mara** was nominated for a Primetime Emmy award for her role in *House of Cards*.

3. Elvis Costello performed "**Radio Radio**" on the 25th anniversary show of *Saturday Night Live*.

4. **Andorra la Vella** means "Andorra the Old" in Catalan.

5. **King Henry VIII**: The pie hid the deeds to English manors.

6. **South Africa**: The Rhodesian Ridgeback breed was developed to hunt lions.

7. **Bill Lee** was used almost exclusively as a relief pitcher during the first 4 years of his MLB career.

8. **Lynn Swann**: President Kennedy changed the name to the President's Council on Physical Fitness to address all age groups.

9. **Robert Cray**, a blues musician, played the bass player in *Animal House*.

10. **Chicago**: *Good Times* was a spin-off of *Maude*, which was itself a spin-off of *All in the Family*.

_____Correct

QUIZ 51 ANSWERS

1. **Eric Taylor:** *Friday Night Lights* is based on the book of the same name by H. G. Bissinger that was published in 1990.

2. Michelangelo created *Madonna of the **Stairs*** during the time he was in the school of Lorenzo de Medici.

3. **RZA** is also known as Prince Rakeem, The Rzarector, Bobby Steels, and Bobby Digital.

4. Lefse is a traditional soft Scandinavian flatbread made out of **potatoes.**

5. **1/100th of a second:** In computing, a jiffy is the time lapsed for one tick of the System Timer Interrupt.

6. **MetLife Stadium** opened in April 2010.

7. *Frisky Dingo*: Many programs on Adult Swim are improvisational, experimental, and underground.

8. **Grammys**: In April 1997, Ellen DeGeneres made television history when she revealed on national television that she is a lesbian.

9. Clancy Brown provides the voice for the CGI **Parallax** in the *Green Lantern* film.

10. **31**: Shaun White won his third Olympic gold medal for the Men's Halfpipe event at the 2018 Winter Olympics.

_____Correct

QUIZ 52 ANSWERS

1. **6 Inches:** The bottom of the net of a table tennis table shall be as close as possible to the playing surface.

2. **1977**: *The Mary Tyler Moore Show* premiered in 1970.

3. **With an earthquake**: R.E.M. released their first single "Radio Free Europe" in 1981.

4. Georgia O'Keeffe was married to the illustrious **Alfred Stieglitz**.

5. **Peter I** is the grandson of Tsar Michael Romanov.

6. **"Romeo and Juliet"** is on Rihanna's *Get On* album.

7. **Erythrophile**: All blood cells are produced in the bone marrow.

8. **José Contreras**' nickname "El Titan de Bronze" first belonged to Lt. General Antonio Maceo who led Cuba against Spain.

9. Standing at just 978 meters high, Scaffel Pike is England's highest peak, found in the **Lake District** in the northwest.

10. Rob Reiner played veteran director **Marty DiBergi** who sets out to film one of England's loudest bands.

_____Correct

QUIZ 53 ANSWERS

1. **Meyers and Carvey:** *SNL* has been the highest rated late-night show in America since 1977.

2. During **"the agony of the leaves,"** tea leaves give themselves to the water and their flavor evolves.

3. Cecil Rhodes was the most famous miner during the South African **diamond** rush in the 1860s.

4. **5-yard Penalty:** A NFL player may only enter the field during a dead ball and must leave crossing his own sideline.

5. **The Beastie Boys** became the third rap group to enter the Rock & Roll Hall of Fame after Run-D.M.C. and Grandmaster Flash and the Furious Five.

6. **Jack Russell Terrier:** In *Frasier*'s first season, Kelsey Grammer won the Emmy Award for Outstanding Lead Actor in a Comedy Series and a People's Choice Award.

7. Starbucks bought the **Tazo** Tea Company in 1999 for 8.1 million dollars.

8. In 2012 and 2017, **Viola Davis** was listed by *TIME* magazine as one of the 100 most influential people in the world.

9. In the early 2000s, Bill Gates reported that he personally wrote the **spam** protection on his office computer.

10. **France:** The Fauvism movement in art lasted only 3 years from 1905–1907.

_____Correct

QUIZ 54 ANSWERS

1. Bada Bing!, a strip club owned Silvio Dante on *The Sopranos*, is an actual strip club on Route 17 in Lodi, New Jersey.

2. **Quiet Riot** was the first heavy metal band to top the pop charts.

3. **Expressionism** refers to art that expresses intense emotion and "being alive."

4. Philip of **Spain** initiated construction of the immense Escorial Palace in 1563 using wealth acquired in the New World.

5. Proxima Centauri (**Alpha Centauri C**), the star closest to Earth, is one of the 3 stars that make up the Alpha Centauri system.

6. Ferdinand's statement on seeing Miranda in *The Tempest*, "O brave new world that has such creatures in it," gave Aldous Huxley his title.

7. **17**: Kobe Bryant was picked thirteenth overall in the 1996 draft.

8. **Jack Black** also voices the monsters Slappy the ventriloquist dummy and the invisible boy in the film.

9. **Hotwired:** Many websites are free to use because they are supported by the revenue from banner ads and, more recently, text ads.

10. In **skiing**, a "daffy" is a midair split in which one ski is pointed down and the other up.

_____Correct

QUIZ 55 ANSWERS

1. **The first sled resembled a skeleton**. Skeleton was an event at the 1928 and 1948 Winter Olympics, then didn't appeared again until the 2002 Winter Olympics in Salt Lake City.

2. **9–12 pints:** Blood is the fluid of life, transporting oxygen from the lungs to body tissue and carbon dioxide from body tissue to the lungs.

3. **Bell tower**: In 1999, the Leaning Tower of Pisa was straightened by 16 inches to keep it from falling over completely.

4. *Two and a Half Men*: Charlie Sheen is the son of Martin Sheen.

5. **Canada**: Neil Young has played with the bands Crazy Horse and The Bluenotes.

6. **Robert Browning** eloped with Elizabeth Barrett (Browning) on September 12, 1846.

7. **Jamaica** receives more than one million visitors per year.

8. **Orange**: In billiards, a red ball must be sunk between each colored ball.

9. **The tobacco mosaic virus** is a plant virus.

10. **Cpl. Hicks**: Michael Biehn has appeared in both *Aliens* and *The Terminator*.

_____Correct

QUIZ 56 ANSWERS

1. McConaughey won the Academy Award for Best Actor for his role as Ron Woodroof in the 2013 film *Dallas Buyers Club*.

2. In 1990 and 1991, **311** released 3 records on their own independent record label, What Have You Records.

3. **Pablo Picasso's father** was a painter who specialized in naturalistic depictions of birds and other game.

4. The United States does not recognize **Argentina**'s claims of sovereignty to the Falkland Islands.

5. The ocean contains 97 percent of the Earth's **water**.

6. Because feathers are brittle, synthetic shuttlecocks have been developed that replace the feathers with a plastic **skirt**.

7. The **bergamot orange** is a pear-shaped, fragrant citrus fruit.

8. **24:** The daytime version of *Wheel of Fortune* aired from January 1975 until September 1991.

9. **Richard Melville Hall**: Moby's great-great-granduncle, Herman Melville, is author of *Moby Dick*.

10. Late in 2009, financial analysts predicted that **Macy's** would likely file bankruptcy again.

_____Correct

QUIZ 57 ANSWERS

1. **Principal Figgins:** Iqbal Theba was born in Karachi, Pakistan.

2. **Michael Kelley:** In *House of Cards* season 3, Doug Stamper's niece and nephew on the show are played by his children in real life.

3. **Anna Paquin** won an Oscar for her role in Jane Campion's *The Piano*.

4. **Peter Griffin**: *Family Guy* first went on the air in 1999.

5. "Now I know! **And knowing is half the battle**. GI-Joe!" was said at the end of every show.

6. **1987**: *Max Headroom* started as a Coke commercial.

7. **Carol Burnett** filed a lawsuit against 20th Century Fox, claiming copyright infringement for her "Charwoman" cleaning character.

8. **A car**: Yau-Man Chan became the final member of the *Survivor: Fiji* jury when Dreamz Herd went back on his word not to vote for him.

9. **Jane and Maura**: Angie Harmon stars as Detective Jane Rizzoli in *Rizzoli & Isles*.

10. **Burn Gorman** played Karl Tanner in the HBO series *Game of Thrones*.

_____Correct

QUIZ 58 ANSWERS

1. Jon Lovitz was a member of the **Saturday Night Live** ensemble from 1985 until 1990.

2. Adele's "**Rolling in the Deep**" won Best Track at the 2011 Q Awards.

3. **Arab oil embargo**: In December 1973, President Carter announced that the National Christmas Tree would not be lit because of the energy crisis.

4. **White**: Beluga calves are gray.

5. The badminton net is 5 feet 1 inch high at the sidelines and **5 feet** high at the center.

6. **Active 60 minutes a day, 5 days a week**: You can earn the Presidential Active Lifestyle Award by meeting your daily activity goal.

7. **Wine and tarragon**: Hollandaise sauce is a key ingredient in Eggs Benedict.

8. **Badly**: Magritte said, "The mind loves images whose meanings are unknown since the meaning of the mind itself is unknown."

9. **Laos**: The tagline for the 2006 movie *Rescue Dawn* was "A true story of survival... declassified."

10. **Marin Cilic** beat Kei Nishikori at the 2014 US Open final.

_____Correct

QUIZ 59 ANSWERS

1. Ramirez replaced Gidget Gein in **Marilyn Manson** in 1994.

2. *That '70s Show*: Topher Grace was in *Mona Lisa Smile* and *Traffic*.

3. Salvador Dali made a number of works that were heavily influenced by **Pablo Picasso** and Joan Miró.

4. **Wahoo**: "Ono" is the Hawaiian word for delicious.

5. The **hurley** measures between 70 to 100 cm long with a flattened, curved end that provides the striking surface.

6. **330,000:** The Earth's magnetic field has boundaries but doesn't fade into space.

7. **53:** The first documented use of the word "nerd" was in a Dr. Seuss story.

8. A part of the **blood supply to the brain** that forms a circle is known as the "circle of Willis."

9. **September 24, 1869:** Jay Gould's scheme to corner the gold market caused a stock market crash called "Black Friday."

10. **John Kane's** art was displayed at the 1927 Carnegie International Exhibition.

_____Correct

QUIZ 60 ANSWERS

1. **Tom Cruise**'s first wife was actress Mimi Rogers.

2. **Ola Ray** also had parts in two Eddie Murphy movies, *Beverly Hills Cops II* and *48 Hours*.

3. **Public Buildings**: Diego Rivera's large wall paintings helped establish the Mexican Mural Renaissance.

4. Due to the writing on his door, Winnie the Pooh was said to live "under the name of **Sanders**."

5. **Plants**: Phytotoxins are used primarily for weed control.

6. **Tony Bennet**: Game 5 of the 2015 World Series was played at Citi Field in New York.

7. **23**: In 2003 at the age of 18 LeBron James became only the second high schooler to be picked first in the NBA draft.

8. The coat of arms of **Havana**, Cuba, bears the appellation "Key to the New World and Rampart of the West Indies" in Spanish.

9. **Black, white, and gray**: Pablo Picasso's *Guernica* was hanging in Madrid's Reina Sofia Museum when it opened in 1992.

10. Martin Scorsese cast directors **Rob Reiner**, Spike Jonze, and Jon Favreau in acting roles.

_____Correct

QUIZ 61 ANSWERS

1. ***The Shape of Water*** had 7 movie nominations at the Golden Globe Awards.

2. **Angelou**'s first book, written in 1969 and titled *I Know Why the Caged Bird Sings*, tells of her life up to the age of 17.

3. **17 feet**: Michelangelo was given the official contract to carve a statue of David on August 16, 1501.

4. **South Pacific**: The Cook Islands, part of New Zealand, were named after British explorer James Cook, who landed there in 1773.

5. **Paul Molitor** is a member of the Baseball Hall of Fame.

6. When **Standard Oil** was broken up by the U.S. government, it formed 34 different oil companies.

7. After **Patio Diet Cola** received positive reviews when introduced in 1963, it was reintroduced as Diet Pepsi in 1964.

8. ***Apollo 8*** was the first human spaceflight to leave the orbit of the Earth.

9. **Hunting**: Herrings turn red after curing and are used to teach hunting dogs to follow a trail.

10. **Slaghoople**: *The Flintstones* was created by the legendary duo of Hanna and Barbera, who were also responsible for *Tom and Jerry*.

_____Correct

QUIZ 62 ANSWERS

1. ***Who Wants to Be a Millionaire?*** has aired in more than 100 countries, making it the most popular television franchise of all time.

2. **Robert De Niro**: *Cape Fear* was actor Gregory Peck's last theatrical film.

3. **John Mayall's Bluesbreakers**: Mick Taylor was inducted into the Rock & Roll Hall of Fame with The Rolling Stones in 1989.

4. **Mata Hari** means "eye of dawn" in Indonesian.

5. A stir was caused when Mets closer Billy Wagner started coming out to Mariano Rivera's signature "**Enter Sandman**."

6. **The bus**: Much of Frida Kahlo's work is influenced by indigenous Mexican culture.

7. **Scripophily**: Some old stock certificates can have considerable value as collector's items.

8. Regular Snapple teas have **blue** caps, white teas have silver caps, and red teas have brushed metal caps.

9. **Ho Ho** isn't just something Santa says, it's a two-handed handplant in snowboarding, which made its Olympic debut in 1998.

10. **Technetium** has an atomic number of 43.

_____Correct

QUIZ 63 ANSWERS

1. **Circle and square**: Leonardo da Vinci's *Vitruvian Man* has been reproduced on everything from the euro to books to t-shirts.

2. **Joey**: In 1991, Matt Leblanc appeared on *Married with Children* as Kelly Bundy's dim boyfriend.

3. George Michael's "**Faith**" reached #1 on the *Billboard* Hot 100 and #2 on the U.K. charts.

4. In order to appear as if he had been imprisoned, Daniel Day-Lewis lost 30 pounds for *In the Name of the Father*.

5. In soil science, **humus** is organic matter that is stable and will not break down.

6. **The Featherie**: The Gutta Percha golf ball, or "Gutta," was created from the dried sap of the sapodilla tree.

7. The Caribbean island of **Saint-Martin**/Saint Maarten in the Lesser Antilles, part French and part Dutch, is the smallest area shared by 2 nations.

8. The first Wendy's restaurant was opened in Columbus, **Ohio,** on November 15, 1969.

9. **Shapes**: The Greek alphabet was developed during the Geometric period, circa 900 to 700 BC.

10. **Albuquerque** is the state of New Mexico's largest city; it sits in the high desert.

_____Correct

QUIZ 64 ANSWERS

1. **The Killers** are from Las Vegas, Nevada.

2. In *The Avengers*, the **Tesseract** is capable of opening a portal to other parts of the universe.

3. **David Arquette** checked into rehab for treatment of "alcohol and other issues" on January 1, 2011, shortly after celebrating New Year's Eve.

4. **Size 22**: Shaquille O'Neal played a genie in the 1996 movie *Kazaam*.

5. **Crocodilia**: American crocodiles are less aggressive than Nile or Australian crocodiles.

6. **Eva Perón** was both a radio and movie actress before she gained political power in Argentina.

7. **March 2003**: The Oxford English Dictionary requires a word to be well established in spoken and written communication before it is added to the dictionary; as new computer words are coined, they often make their way into the OED.

8. **Richard Nixon** was the 37th president of the United States.

9. **Dantes**: *The Count of Monte Cristo* was a novel written by Alexandre Dumas.

10. **TKO**: Ronda Rousey defeated Sara McMann by TKO as a result of a knee to the body.

_____Correct

QUIZ 65 ANSWERS

1. The **Photorealism** art movement began in the United States in the late 1960s and early 1970s.

2. Drew Cary took over as the host of ***The Price Is Right*** in the fall of 2007.

3. **Holy Trinity**: Dwyane Wade is a Christian and tithes 10 percent of his salary to a local church in Chicago.

4. **Ezekiel 25**: Samuel L. Jackson played the hit man Jules in *Pulp Fiction*.

5. **Destiny's Child**'s Kelly Rowland's debut album *Simply Deep* was released in 2002.

6. **2000**: Hollister Co. is under the management of Abercrombie & Fitch.

7. **Snap** first appeared on Rice Krispies boxes in 1933, while Crackle, Pop, and the later-dropped Pow came in 1941.

8. **Neuschwanstein Castle** was built by Ludwig the II of Bavaria as a place to withdraw from public life.

9. **Pedro Martinez**: The first Cy Young Award was given in 1956.

10. Because **Larry King** voiced the part of a female barmaid, some groups boycotted *Shrek 2* for promoting "transgenderism."

_____Correct

QUIZ 66 ANSWERS

1. A **Banana Republic** was lampooned in Woody Allen's 1971 movie *Bananas*.

2. Most **78** records were 3 to 5 minutes per side.

3. **Gus Grissom** was the second American to fly in space.

4. **A mural** is any piece of artwork painted or applied directly on a wall, ceiling, or other permanent surface.

5. The most influential **first-person shooter** game was Doom, which was released in 1993.

6. The **Zapruder film** was purchased by *Life* magazine for $150,000.

7. **Clams** live in the sand upside down.

8. Male **ducks** are called drakes while female ducks are called hens.

9. **Alcatraz** functioned as a federal prison from 1935 through 1963.

10. **Arugula** is a form of lettuce.

_____Correct

QUIZ 67 ANSWERS

1. **Hoboken, New Jersey,** on the appropriately named Elysian Fields.

2. **Ansel Adams** pioneered the Zone System as a way to determine proper exposure and adjust the contrast of the final print.

3. The first 50 titles were *released* in **Japan** on October 1, 1982.

4. **Budokan** was originally built for the judo competition in the 1964 Summer Olympics.

5. *Interiors* received 5 Academy Award nominations.

6. Some **parrots** can live for over 80 years.

7. **Burnishing:** The earliest surviving substantive illuminated manuscripts are from the period 400 to 600 A.D.

8. **George Michael**'s *Faith* album sold over 20 million copies worldwide.

9. **Alaska** has more than 3 million lakes.

10. The seldom-used term is **tittle**.

_____Correct

QUIZ 68 ANSWERS

1. Julia Roberts did her cameo in **The Player** for nothing.

2. **Michael Bay** originally turned down the offer to direct *Transformers* as he felt it was "a stupid toy movie."

3. **Laurence Fishburn**: *The Matrix* employed never-before-used special effects specially designed for the movie.

4. Barack and Michelle Obama saw **Do the Right Thing** on their first date in 1989.

5. **Gary Oldman**: *Sid and Nancy* featured an appearance by Courtney Love.

6. **Shark Tale**.

7. **Suicide Bomber**: *Contact* is a 1997 sci-fi film starring Jodie Foster.

8. Vince says specifically that his car was out **5 days** when it was keyed.

9. The Brooklyn Dodgers won the World Series at **Ebbets Field** in 1955.

10. **Kip Thorne** was an executive producer and scientific consultant on *Interstellar*.

_____Correct

QUIZ 69 ANSWERS

1. **Donald**: Frances Bean Cobain is the daughter of Nirvana's Kurt Cobain and Courtney Love.

2. The Black Keys named their seventh studio album after the **El Camino** muscle car but the cover art depicts a minivan.

3. Columbia Records executive John Hammond signed **Bob Dylan** to his first recording contract.

4. "**Comfortably Numb**" has been covered by artists as diverse as Graham Parker, Dar Williams, and Scissor Sisters.

5. Former Minnesota Governor Jesse Ventura played "**Werewolves of London**" at his inauguration party.

6. **Browne and Frey**: Jackson Browne later recorded "Take It Easy" and included it on his second album *For Everyman*.

7. *Is Is*: A song featuring vocals by Karen O. of The Yeah Yeah Yeahs was used in a 2005 Nike commercial.

8. The Arctic Monkeys played "**Do I Wanna Know?**" as the opening number throughout the AM Tour.

9. **Modest Mouse**'s first single was released on Calvin Johnson's K Records.

10. **Neutral Milk Hotel** released their best-known and most critically acclaimed album *In the Aeroplane Over the Sea* in 1998.

_____Correct

QUIZ 70 ANSWERS

1. **Collages**.

2. Italian Filippo Tomasso Marinetti was the founder of the **Futurism** Art movement.

3. Frida Kahlo conveyed personal and physical pain through her expressive **self-portraits**.

4. **Piet Mondrian**'s *Broadway Boogie-Woogie* was highly influential in the school of abstract geometric painting.

5. *Wheatfield with Crows*: From his cell in the asylum at Saint-Rémy, Vincent van Gogh could see wheatfields and this inspired his series of wheatfield paintings.

6. Favrile glass is a kind of **iridescent** art glass that was created by Louis Comfort Tiffany.

7. **The Present**: Pablo Picasso painted in many styles during his lifetime including still life, classicism, surrealism, and cubism.

8. Late in his life **Degas** turned to modeling statues in wax.

9. During his 5 years at the Royal **Tapestry** Workshop, Goya create 42 different patterns.

10. **Jean Dubuffet** first used the term "assemblage" to describe a method of turning objects into 3-dimensional structures.

_____Correct

QUIZ 71 ANSWERS

1. Rockefeller made his fortune in the **oil** industry.

2. **40.**

3. **Reno, Nevada,** is near the border of northern California and farther west than either Los Angeles or Fresno.

4. **Nothing**: Unable to decide on a middle name, Truman's parents simply went with "S."

5. **Under God.**

6. **Squirrel Nut Zippers** is an old-fashioned peanut-and-caramel candy.

7. **John Wayne**, the hero in many military films, did not serve in the military.

8. **The octopus** has 3 hearts, one for its body and one for each of its gills.

9. *Mr. Buchanan's Administration on the Eve of Rebellion*, published in 1866, was 17th President **James Buchanan's** look back on his time in office.

10. *Guernica* is considered one of Picasso's masterpieces.

_____Correct

QUIZ 72 ANSWERS

1. **Cobras.**

2. Jem is forced to read to the dying **Mrs. Dubose** after he destroys her flower garden.

3. **Austria.**

4. **Aroldis Chapman** delivered the pitch on September 24, 2010, against the San Diego Padres.

5. **The Fujita Scale** is used to measure the wind speed of tornadoes.

6. Meteoroids are particles that become meteoroids once they **enter an atmosphere**.

7. **80.**

8. In adults, **lead poisoning** can lead to high blood pressure, nerve disorders, joint pain, and infertility.

9. **Jack Nicklaus** holds the record with a total of 18 championships.

10. On **Nashville Skyline**, Dylan and Cash performed "Girl from the North Country."

_____Correct